ENTERTAINING INDIAN-STYLE

ENTERTAINING INDIAN-STYLE

Shehzad Husain

Photographs by Eric Carter

TREASURE PRESS

Author's dedication
With love to Mummy and my late Pappa

First published in Great Britain in 1985 by
Columbus Books
This edition published in 1989 by
Treasure Press
Michelin House
81 Fulham Road
London SW3 6RB

ISBN 1 85051 399 6

Printed in Hong Kong

Contents

CHAPTER 1

An Indian Invitation

The subcontinent of India and Pakistan covers some 4 million square kilometres and comprises very many different cultures and religions, of which the main groups are the Hindus and the Muslims, within each of which are smaller sects, the Parsees and the Christians. All of these have influenced the eating habits and tastes of the various ethnic communities throughout the subcontinent. The food eaten in the north, for example, differs considerably from that of the south. The people of the north, which is a wheat-growing area, prefer Indian breads such as *chapatis* or *paratas* as their staple, while rice, which is grown in many of the southern states, is preferred by the southerners.

Muslims are the meat-eating population of India, but for religious reasons they do not eat anything derived from the pig, which is considered unclean. Hindus, a vast majority of whom are vegetarians, are forbidden to eat beef, because the cow is considered to be a sacred animal.

Spices and herbs have been used to flavour food for thousands of years in the East, and India has for centuries been an important source of spices for Western nations. Yet it is only in the last twenty years or so that the majority of people in the West have become generally aware of our spicy cuisine. This may well be due in part to the great ease of communication, by jet travel, with India, and the fact that many people are now travelling to the Indian subcontinent where they have the opportunity to taste a variety of dishes on their home ground. But most of all it has been due to the proliferation of Indian restaurants in towns and cities throughout the world and, in particular, the British Isles. The Indian communities which have settled in Britain and in other countries have not only preserved their own culture and eating habits but, through setting up their own trading systems for specialist ingredients, made real Indian cookery possible on a far wider scale than would have been thought possible even, say, ten years ago.

While the Indian people do not generally learn to cook from cookery books, but by family example using recipes that are handed down from generation to generation, non-Indians who have acquired a taste for our food usually need some guidance. Whether or not you have done any Indian cookery before, you will find that most of the recipes in this book are very straightforward and need no specialist skills or experience to be successfully carried out.

This book is of course directed in particular towards Indian cookery for entertaining, though you will undoubtedly want to use your favourite recipes on other occasions when you are not entertaining as well. Entertaining Indian-style has certain advantages for the cook: Indian dishes are wonderfully good-tempered, in that very few of them need any last-minute attention whatsoever (maybe just sprinkling with a garnish in some cases); the majority of the dishes can be made well in advance and will freeze very happily – and indeed, some actually improve through keeping; others will usually wait in a refrigerator for a day or so until you are ready to re-heat them; this means that the cook, provided she has planned her meal carefully, can join her guests for a drink before the meal without the slightest worry about what might be happening in the kitchen. Also, because it is perfectly correct to serve all the dishes, other than the dessert, at once, she need not leap up from the first course in order to get the main course organized – everything can go on the table at the beginning of the meal.

I discovered as a teacher of Indian cookery that my students' main reason for wanting to learn to cook Indian-style was because they wanted to produce these dishes for their partners and their friends, who all love Indian food. It seems that Indian cooking is virtually guaranteed to score a hit with everyone. And if you have one vegetarian guest among a gathering of meat-eaters, Indian cuisine, with its *dhaals* and other delicious vegetarian dishes, can often solve your problem for you.

What about the question of spiciness? Must you spend a fortune on a cupboard full of exotic items before you even begin? And how do you gauge what degree of 'hotness' will be acceptable to your guests? Almost all the recipes contain spices of one sort or another, but not necessarily a wide selection for each individual dish. Some curries, for example, require just two types of spice, another might need a combination of, say, twelve different herbs and spices. However, if you know you like Indian food and are likely to be cooking it on a regular basis, it is advisable to buy a basic range of spices for your own convenience (see page 26) which will see you through a good variety of recipes. Then build up gradually as you start to try others. 'Hotness' often depends on the amount of chilli, in whatever form: fresh chillis, which I use a great deal for garnish as well as in curry sauces, dried chillis and ground chilli (chilli powder, also known as cayenne). It is as well to under- rather than over-estimate the amount of chilli you will need until you gain some experience in Indian cooking, and to remember that you can take some of the sting out of chilli pods by scraping out the seeds. But, most importantly, do not make the mistake of thinking that all Indian curries must be red-hot to be 'authentic'. They need not be, and moreover we usually serve a variety of mild and hot dishes at any given meal. You should always plan your meals to include both mild and hotter dishes, because there is no point in destroying your guests' palates for your more delicately-flavoured dishes by killing their taste buds with chilli.

The dishes in Indian meals, as I have already said, are not served in any specific order, other than the fact that dessert is always served last. We rarely have soup, and starters as such do not really exist. However, some restaurants serve kebabs, for example, and tandoori chicken (chicken spiced and marinated in yoghurt, then cooked in a clay oven) as starters, and you can certainly do so if you wish to split the meal up into more courses. In most Indian households, a complete meal would consist of one meat or chicken dish, one vegetarian dish, a *raita* (yoghurt sauce with either onions, mint or cucumber), *dhaal* (any type of lentil, either cooked in a sauce or dry) with rice or *chapati*. All these are set out on the table at the same time.

Entertaining in India itself is a little different in certain respects from Western-style entertaining. For a start, it usually means a far bigger guest list. While in the West one couple might invite another couple or two for dinner, this would be unusual in India. Whether the occasion is a family celebration or a gathering for a religious festival, parents always bring their children; also, as families tend to be much more closely-knit, there is far greater mixing of the generations and of non-immediate family members.

When I was a child in Karachi, whenever we had a party or were invited to one there were usually thirty to fifty people, including the children, and invitations normally extended to entire families. Now that I host parties myself I find that the numbers are often smaller, but for dinner parties I tend to invite about six to eight couples at a time, as the greater quantity of food required does not seem to make a great deal of difference to the time spent in preparation.

For a recent birthday of my husband's, I decided to give him a surprise party, and by the time I had finished with the guest list I had forty adults plus about a dozen children! Yet I was absolutely determined to keep it a secret, even from my parents-in-law who were staying with us at the time. I started the preparation about a week in advance, making items such as kebabs and *dhaals* and freezing them. The previous day I prepared a prawn curry and chicken *khorma*, and I cooked a vegetable *pulao* and *paratas* (bread) about two hours before the guests arrived.

My husband, like most Indian men, likes good food but does not know the first thing about cooking — which helped, in a way, because he caught me cutting a tray full of onions and asked me why I was chopping up so many. (I told him I had invited a couple over for Sunday lunch.)

In all, the menu consisted of about eight different items, and I must admit that it was a lot of hard work even with the help of modern appliances such as the food processor. I also made full use of the refrigerator, freezer, oven and electric 'hostess' trolley — and the surprise party worked extremely well, with a wonderful time had by all.

This was far from being the largest number for which I have ever catered. A few years ago, we decided to have some people to the house to celebrate a Muslim ceremony called a *bismillah* (held to mark the occasion when a child starts to read the Muslim holy book, the Quran, in Arabic, usually at about the age of four or four-and-a-half). When we sat down to prepare a guest list what had begun as 'having a few people over' soon became a gathering of eighty people, counting the children. As our house could not accommodate so many, we decided to hire a restaurant, but as I wanted to do part of the catering myself this took a little time and patience to arrange. Eventually a London restaurant agreed to work with me in this way: their chefs would supply a lamb biryani and a chicken *khorma*, with *raita* and other trimmings and the drinks, while I would bring from home *shaami* kebabs (page 81), pea and potato curry (page 68), an aubergine dish called *bagaray baingun* and two desserts — a fruit trifle and a carrot halva.

Preparation began a week in advance with the cooking and freezing of the *shaami* kebabs. Then, two days before, I cooked the aubergine dish and the carrot halva; the pea and potato curry and about ten bowls of trifle were prepared on the same day. I thoroughly enjoyed the cooking, though it was hard work; looking back, the worst part was taking the food to the restaurant — sitting in the car, clad in a beautiful silk saree and wearing heavy jewellery, with the greasy pots and pans! I am sure it was all worth while, though, because everything went exactly as planned and the guests seemed to appreciate the meal very much indeed.

Perhaps you are wondering where my love of cooking began. In one respect it is a little strange, because when I was a young child in India my sister and I were hardly allowed into the kitchen. We were fortunate enough then to have servants, and it was assumed that we would marry into households where there would be plenty of staff to do all the chores. It did not quite work out like that, but I am not sorry because I have always loved cooking and it has become one of the great interests of my life. As a very young girl, I remember in particular that Sundays, when all the relatives from both my mother's and my father's family used to visit us, gave me the opportunity for my first practical experiences of cooking. We children with our cousins used to erect a small tent in the garden, and over a small cast-iron stove, a bit like a barbecue, called an *anghetih*, we would cook some fried rice and lentils (known as *kitcheri*) in ghee and spices in earthenware pots. We would eat this while the grown-ups had a variety of 'proper' dishes (full-scale curries) and snacks for tea. We found it thrilling to be allowed to cook something for ourselves.

Among my other memories of India that have influenced this book are the picnics that we used to go on with our friends and relations. As the sun in India is so hot, we would wait for a nice cloudy day to go to the beach or picnic park. We used to hire a van so that everyone could sit together and my uncles and aunts would sing and play the harmonium all the way to the picnic spot.

Food was, as always, an important element of the occasion. My mother would organize a number of items such as *paratas* (bread), *kheema* (dry curry) and *shaami* kebabs — the latter were a must, being a favourite with everyone and also conveniently dry and easy to carry.

Our picnic baskets used to be extremely heavy, I recall, because paper plates and cups were not so easily available in those days, and we would always make sure a hut was available where the ladies could organize the food, tea and other drinks.

When I was about six years old my father, who was an entomologist, was offered a job by the Sudanese government. He accepted the position and arranged that my mother, brothers and sisters and I would join him after a year. It was a courageous thing for him to do, as he knew very little about the Sudan apart from the fact that it had just got its independence from the British. A year passed, and my mother, the rest of my family and I boarded a ship from Bombay. As my mother did not know what to expect on her arrival, we took with us everything we could think of that might be necessary – including all the spices we would need to cook the Indian dishes we enjoyed at home. My mother also decided to take her nanny with us. She was like a grandmother to all of us and we all loved her dearly. (She was also a great cook, and some of the recipes in this book were passed on to me by her.)

I will never forget how exciting it was to board the ship; we had booked three cabins, but ended up all sleeping in the same cabin every night, partly because my mother was afraid that one of my brothers would sleepwalk! My mother made very good friends with the captain of the ship when she discovered that he, like us, was from Hyderabad and his family was also on board. So even on the ship, if my mother requested dishes such as *thill ki chutney* (sesame seed chutney) or lamb biryani, she got them.

Finally we reached our new home, in a small town called Wad Medani, where the spices we had brought proved extremely useful. What I remember most vividly about the food we had in the Sudan, however, is the delicious meals that my Nan cooked and the huge water melons and other lovely tropical fruits that we used to have after them. Even now, I like to serve these after a spicy and filling meal – there is nothing more refreshing.

After a few years in the Sudan my parents decided that for the sake of our education it would be better if they moved to England, so I suppose it was at this stage, when I was about twelve, that they decided to uproot. It was when I started school in England that I began to learn to cook (English dishes) properly. I used to come home with things like shortbread and the odd sponge cake, and I sometimes made these at weekends at home, too. It used to please my mother immensely that I was beginning to show a real interest in cookery, so at about this time she started to teach me to cook – though at the time, she was little more than a novice herself, in fact, having grown up in India with servants to take care of all the family's meals as well as the household chores. She had had to write home for recipes and information about cookery techniques and more or less teach herself. She had not found it very easy to learn to cook in this way, and she was determined that I would not have to experience the same difficulties. And so, realizing that the sooner I learned to cook the better it would be for me, she started to train me. I began with simple dishes such as the *kheema* on page 40 (minced lamb with peas), and with basic spices such as ginger, garlic and chilli powder. As my interest grew, I gradually became more adventurous, and before long Sunday had become my day for cooking.

When I married, I was very nervous about cooking for my husband for the first time, however, because he was from northern India and I was from the south, where we tend to like dishes hotter and to serve them with rice rather than bread. I need not have been nervous, though, because it has been his appreciation and encouragement since our marriage that have spurred me on, and which has in fact widened both our horizons and tastes. His mother has introduced me to many dishes which I might not otherwise have known about, including the very hot lamb curry (*nehari*) that is traditionally eaten at breakfast.

Of all the reasons for entertaining, weddings must surely be the most important in any culture, and Indian culture is no exception. Perhaps the full-scale Indian or Pakistani wedding is the most impressive of all, however, because it can last a week to ten days, culminating in the marriage ceremony itself. It means many formal dinners, for a guest list of anything from two hundred to well over a thousand people (a hundred or more a day), and a vast amount of effort by all concerned except for the bride and groom, who are not expected to take part in any of the chores and can therefore have a relaxing time. Usually there is a houseful of friends and relations on both sides; the house is decorated with coloured lights, a colourfully printed marquee, a *shamiana*, is erected, and there are fresh flowers everywhere. The women of the house normally sit together and plan the menus in advance. As the food must be different every night this requires a great deal of imagination, but chicken or lamb biryani is always a must at weddings – probably because these include saffron, the most expensive spice in the world. The dinners before the wedding day might consist of kebabs, *paratas* (bread) with halva or *subzee pulao* (vegetable pulao) and a combination of curries. It is not uncommon to hire *bawarchis*, professional chefs, for the actual cooking, so that the women can take part in the festivities.

Many receptions are now held at hotels, but for the days leading up to this banquet there is still a vast number of guests to be catered for daily at either the bride's or the groom's home, depending on where the ceremony is being held on that particular evening. What must seem very strange and unfair to Western people is the fact that the bride does not leave home during the celebrations, though of course her presence is required for the marriage ceremony, wherever that may be taking place.

The guests, as well as the bride and groom and their families, plan their clothes well in advance. The women make the most of the opportunity to wear a different saree and jewellery each night, and fresh flowers in their hair. As for the bride, in our community (the Hyderabadis) she wears bright red, with gold embroidery. Her clothes, together with her jewellery and accessories, are bought by the groom's family. It is also customary for the bride to wear henna on her hands and feet, drawn on in beautiful patterns by a woman who is called in specially for this purpose. The same woman will also draw henna designs on the hands of the women guests after finishing her work on the bride. (I remember when I was a bride how difficult it was to keep still for four or five hours after the henna paste had been applied in order to let it dry.) Afterwards, the paste is washed off, leaving an intricate design which lasts for about two weeks.

The groom normally wears a loose shirt made of silk and a long brocade jacket, and is garlanded with fresh flowers – roses, especially, in Muslim communities, and also jasmine.

At the wedding of one of my cousins recently, held on the lawns of a large club, there were 1200 guests, and besides an army of chefs and waiters many of the guests provided help in one way or another. The menu for the dinner, held out of doors after the wedding ceremony on a beautiful moonlit July night, consisted of lamb biryani, *shaami* kebabs, *bagaray baingun* (pickled aubergines), and both a chicken and a lamb *khorma*, accompanied by *raita* (yoghurt sauce) and *naan* (yeasted bread). This was followed by a dessert of either ice cream or *shahi tukray*, which is an Indian bread pudding with saffron and almonds. Excellent as it was, after a week of such rich food we were looking forward to something very simple, like plain boiled rice or *chapati* and vegetable curry, which just goes to show that you can indeed have too much of a good thing.

Though I suspect that you might not be tackling anything on quite the scale of this wedding banquet, at least to begin with, I would like to wish you many happy hours of cooking and I hope you enjoy entertaining Indian-style.

CHAPTER 2
Meal-planning and Menus

Once you have decided on the date and the guest list for your entertaining, the next step is to plan the menu. Use the sample in the pages that follow as examples, but do not be afraid to change these around or to create your own – or, for that matter, to serve Indian dishes as part of a Western meal. For a completely Indian menu, try to plan the dishes so that you have a variety of main ingredients and so that no two dishes are very similar in appearance, or in taste. I also try to contrast wet and dry dishes. You would also try to avoid having, for example, two yoghurt sauces, or two which contain red (or yellow) colouring; on the other hand, it is a good idea to vary the degree of spiciness, or hotness, in your chosen dishes.

For entertaining, aim to pick four to six different dishes. For authenticity, you should always include a chicken dish (considered to be a delicacy in India). Of course, if you know that one of your guests has a favourite dish – or for that matter dislikes a particular item – that will help you to arrive at a successful formula.

In addition you will want a vegetable dish, a *dhaal* (lentil dish), rice and bread. For a more formal meal the structure would be very similar except that there might be an extra dish, probably a vegetable, and there would certainly be a dessert.

You will notice that there are no soups among my recipes. This is because soups are not really considered to belong to Indian cuisine: they are something the Indians have copied from the English since the days of the Raj.

If you wish to serve a starter, perhaps a chicken tikka, tandoori-style prawns or a kebab dish, present them garnished with a crisp piece of lettuce, onion rings, lemon wedges and maybe a few pieces of cucumber and tomatoes. Some restaurants tend to serve *naans* with the starter, but these are very filling; a lighter choice of 'trimming' would be *raita* (yoghurt sauce), *kachoomer* (onions and tomatoes), or mango chutney.

Alternatively, serve an exotic fruit as a starter: a small piece of water melon or a mixture of several different types of melon would make a light, refreshing prelude to an Indian meal.

When we plan dinner-party menus the rice is always cooked in a special way. Biryani is one possibility, and is considered to be special because it includes the costly spice saffron. The saffron crocus yields bluish-purple flowers each autumn, and the flowers' dried stigmas are marketed both in strands and powdered. Among many other rice dishes suitable for entertaining are *pulao bagara khana* (fried spicy rice) and *subzee pulao*, a vegetable pulao. Plain boiled rice is not considered special, as it is cooked every day in most households. We also provide a *roti* (bread) as well as rice. Ideally, the bread should be eaten first, because rice makes the plate messy; rice and bread should not be eaten at the same time.

If you have chosen, say, a lamb biryani, try to choose a chicken dish to accompany this rather than another lamb dish, to avoid repeating the main ingredient. However, if you were to serve a chicken tikka, which has no sauce, as a starter, and a totally different type of chicken dish as a second meat dish in your main course (say a curry), this would be acceptable. Do not overlook kebabs; served garnished with onion rings and lemon wedges, these look attractive and are always popular.

Poppadums, pickles, salads and chutneys should be included if possible, as these not only add variety to the range of tastes but will make the table more colourful and attractive.

The suggested menus that follow are not rigid formulas: change them round as you wish until you have a meal that appeals to you, avoiding dishes that seem to have too much in common.

I have suggested an Indian dessert for each of the more formal menus, but as these are rather rich and sweet I recommend that you also serve some fresh fruit: mangoes, guavas (if you can find them), papayas, water melon – especially in summer – or any other type of melon would be ideal. Nowadays, fortunately, practically all the exotic fruits appropriate to an Indian meal are available from supermarkets.

During the planning, it is easy to overlook the pre-prandial stage: in India dinner parties usually begin with soft drinks, such as fruit juices, with spicy 'nibbles' to accompany such as spiced roast almonds, or mixtures of rice, nuts, raisins and spices. This book features a few recipes for both drinks and Indian accompaniments. In India you can buy such snacks along the roadside while elsewhere you can either buy them from Indian or Pakistani grocers or make them yourself (pages 124–30). Though fresher and much more satisfying when made at home, they always make a deliciously different accompaniment to an aperitif.

Whether you are catering for a large or a small gathering, if the party is to include children they are likely to enjoy sitting by themselves at a separate table. I usually set one up in the kitchen, if the children are old enough to feed themselves, so that they can enjoy their own private dinner party – and perhaps make a little more noise than would be acceptable from them if they were alongside the adults.

Many of the dishes listed in the menus that follow are shown in the colour photographs that occur throughout the book.

Small dinner parties

The following menus are suitable for informal dinner parties of 4–6 people.

MENU 1	*MAIN COURSE*	Parata (layered bread) Bagara khana (fried spicy rice) Aloo gobi (potato and cauliflower curry) Badaami khorma (lamb curry) Tarka dhaal (oil-dressed lentils) with a fresh salad or Kachoomer (onions and tomatoes in lemon juice)
	DESSERT	Fresh fruit
MENU 2	*MAIN COURSE*	Chapati (unleavened bread) Khushka (plain boiled rice) Bhindi bhujia (okra curry) Kheema matar (minced lamb with peas) Khatti dhaal (lemon dhaal) Aam ki chutney (mango chutney)
MENU 3	*MAIN COURSE*	Poori (deep-fried bread) Dahi ki kadi (dumplings in yoghurt sauce) Nargisi kofteh (meat-coated eggs) Aloo matar (potatoes and peas) Kheeray ki salad (cucumber salad)

Special anniversary dinners

These menus are for two people, and would make a memorable meal for a candlelight dinner to celebrate a birthday.

MENU 1	*STARTER*	Tandoori-style prawns (with parata if desired)
	MAIN COURSE	Naan, bagara khana (yeasted bread, fried spicy rice) Kheema bhare tamatar (stuffed tomatoes) Dahi vale baingun (fried aubergine in yoghurt) Murgh kali mirch (chicken in black pepper)
	SALAD	Kabli chana salad (chick pea salad)
	DESSERT	Gajar ka halva (carrot dessert with fresh cream)

MENU 2	STARTER	Chicken tikka with naan (dry spicy chicken with yeasted bread)
	MAIN COURSE	Pulao rice (rice cooked with saffron and cardamoms, etc.) Dum ka kheema (grilled minced lamb) Prawn tamatar (tomatoes and prawns) Cucumber raita (yoghurt sauce with cucumber)
	SALAD	Gajar aur podinay ka salad (carrot and mint salad)
	DESSERT	Shahi tukray (Indian bread pudding)
MENU 3	STARTER	Boti kebab (boned lamb kebab) with a crisp salad
	MAIN COURSE	Roghni roti (lightly fried bread) Subzee pulao (vegetable pulao rice) Roghan goshth (lamb curry in a thick sauce) Thurai aur methi (courgettes and fresh fenugreek leaves) Mint raita (yoghurt and mint sauce)
	DESSERT	Zarda (sweet saffron rice)

Special dinner parties

These menus feature some of the more impressive dishes from the book, and are for 6–20 people.

MENU 1	MAIN COURSE	Parata (layered bread) Kuchchi yukhni ki biryani (chicken and rice cooked with yoghurt and spices) Dum ka kheema (grilled minced lamb) Roghan goshth (lamb curry cooked in yoghurt, tomatoes and spices) Mooli ka raita (white radish in yoghurt) Lime pickle
	DESSERT	Gulab jamun (deep-fried sweetmeat in syrup) Fresh fruit
MENU 2	MAIN COURSE	Parata (layered bread) Lamb biryani (lamb cooked in yoghurt and spices with rice) Murgh makhani (buttered chicken with a thick sauce) Aloo gobi (potato and cauliflower curry) Chahni huwi dhaal aur kofteh (strained dhaal with meatballs) Masalay dar corn (spicy corn) Kheeray ki salad (cucumber salad)
	DESSERT	Gajar ka halva (carrot dessert) Fresh fruit

MENU 3 *MAIN COURSE* Parata/chapati (layered bread/unleavened bread)
Bagara khana (fried spicy rice)
Chaplee kebabs (minced lamb kebabs with pomegranate seeds)
Dahi ki kadi (dumplings in a yoghurt sauce)
Chicken khorma (chicken cooked in yoghurt)
Hot salad
Baingun raita (aubergines in yoghurt)

DESSERT Shahi tukray (Indian bread pudding with saffron and almonds)
Fresh fruit

MENU 4 *MAIN COURSE* Poori (deep-fried bread)
Pulao (rice cooked with saffron and cardamoms, etc.)
Tandoori chicken (grilled spicy chicken)
Badaami khorma (lamb cooked in yoghurt and almonds)
Dahi vale baingun (fried aubergines in yoghurt)
Masalay vale aloo (spicy potatoes)
Kachoomer (onions and tomatoes in lemon juice)

DESSERT Sheer khorma (Indian vermicelli pudding)
Fresh fruit

MENU 5 *MAIN COURSE* Chapati/poori (unleavened bread/deep-fried bread)
Subzee pulao (vegetable rice)
Tamatar prawns (tomatoes and prawns)
Sabath masala goshth (lamb cooked in whole spices)
Kadahi chicken (deep-fried chicken with tomatoes and peppers)
Bagaray baingun (aubergines in pickling spices)
Cucumber raita (cucumber in yoghurt)

DESSERT Badaam ke lauze (almond slices)
Fresh fruit

MENU 6 *MAIN COURSE* Naan (yeasted bread)
Pulao (rice cooked with saffron and cardamoms, etc.)
Murgh tikka (chicken grilled with yoghurt and spices)
Pasandeh (spicy lamb cooked in yoghurt)
Thalay huway jhingay aur mirch (fried prawns with peppers)
Khatti dhaal or tarka dhaal (lemon or oil-dressed dhaal)
Gajar aur podinay ka salad (carrot and mint salad)

DESSERT Chawal ki kheer (rice pudding)

MENU 7	*MAIN COURSE*	Parata (layered bread)
		Tamatar ka khana (tomato rice)
		Shaami kebabs (meat kebabs)
		Palak aur chanay ki dhaal (spinach and lentils)
		Dum ki murgh (roast chicken pieces in coconut and spices)
		Aloo ka khorma (potatoes cooked with meat in yoghurt)
		Kachoomer (onions and tomatoes in lemon juice)
	DESSERT	Firni (ground rice pudding)
		Fresh fruit

MENU 8	*MAIN COURSE*	Parata (layered bread)
		Bagara khana (fried spicy rice)
		Kheema bhare tamatar (tomatoes stuffed with minced lamb)
		Murgh dopiaza (chicken and onions)
		Boti kebabs (boned lamb kebabs)
		Mint raita (mint in yoghurt)
		Tarka dhaal (oil-dressed dhaal)
	DESSERT	Shakar kand ki kheer (sweet potato dessert)
		Fresh fruit

MENU 9	*MAIN COURSE*	Khichra (lamb cooked with three types of lentil) and trimmings
	DESSERT	Lassi (yoghurt drink)
		Pistay ka halva (pistachio dessert)
		Fresh fruit

MENU 10	*MAIN COURSE*	Raan (lamb pot roast)
		Masalay vale aloo (potatoes with spices and onions)
		Bagara khana (fried spicy rice)
		Gajar aur podinay ka salad (carrot and mint salad)
		Fried corn and peas
	DESSERT	Firni (ground rice pudding)
		Fresh fruit

(I would recommend menu no. 10 if you are entertaining anyone who is not used to eating Indian food.)

Informal parties

These menus feature less elaborate dishes than the preceding set, and are for 6–20 people.

MENU 1
Chapati (unleavened bread)
Khushka (plain boiled rice)
Tamatar ka khorma (tomatoes cooked with meat and yoghurt)
Khadi dhaal (onion dhaal)
Chaplee kebabs (minced lamb kebabs with pomegranate seeds)

MENU 2
Khushka (plain boiled rice)
Parata (layered bread)
Aamchoor ka dopiaza (lamb with onions and dried mango powder)
Khatti dhaal (lemon dhaal)
Thali huwi phool gobi (fried cauliflower)

MENU 3
Chapati (unleavened bread)
Bagara khana (fried spicy rice)
Potato cutlets (mashed potatoes filled with mince and coated with breadcrumbs)
Tamatar ki chutney (tomato curry)
Bhindi bhujia (okra curry)

MENU 4
Bagara khana (fried spicy rice)
Chapati (unleavened bread)
Maya khalia (spicy lamb curry in sauce)
Khadi dhaal (onion dhaal)
Murgh kali mirch (chicken tossed in black pepper)
Kachoomer (onions and tomatoes in lemon juice)

MENU 5
Parata (layered bread)
Tamatar ka khana (tomato rice)
Kheema matar (minced lamb with peas)
Dahi vale baingun (fried aubergines in yoghurt)

MENU 6
Paratas (layered bread)
Khushka (plain boiled rice)
Saag goshth (lamb cooked in spinach)
Tamatar ki chutney (tomato curry)

MENU 7
Kitcheri (spiced rice and lentils)
Shorway vale kheemay kay kofteh (curried meatballs)
Thill ki chutney (sesame seed chutney)
or
Tamatar ki chutney (tomato curry)
Kachoomer (onions and tomatoes in lemon juice)

Vegetarian menus

Like many people I have tried to cut down on my family's fat intake by cooking completely vegetarian meals from time to time, and now do it regularly — about twice a week. To begin with my children missed the meat, but after a while they became accustomed to eating and enjoying vegetarian meals. Now, a visit to a vegetarian restaurant is something to which they happily look forward.

Of course, many, many people are now committed, rather than occasional, vegetarians, and vegetarian food is steadily growing in popularity. Indian dishes can provide some welcome variety in a meatless diet, especially when they incorporate some more unusual vegetables such as okra or aubergines. These two vegetables in particular are far tastier when cooked without meat.

I always try to include a *dhaal* in a vegetarian menu. All lentils have a high protein content, unlike vegetables, and they can therefore replace the protein forfeited when meat is excluded from a meal.

Kachoomer (onions and tomatoes in lemon juice) and mango chutney complement vegetarian meals beautifully, with plain boiled rice, *pooris* or *chapatis*.

To finish, try a halva, rice pudding or semolina dish, or serve fresh fruit as a dessert.

MENU 1	*MAIN COURSE*	Poori (deep-fried bread)
		Khushka (plain boiled rice)
		Bhindi bhujia (okra curry)
		Khatti dhaal (lemon dhaal)
		Subzee ke kebab (vegetable kebabs)
		Kachoomer (onions and tomatoes in lemon juice)
	DESSERT	Gulab jamun (deep-fried sweetmeat in syrup)
MENU 2	*MAIN COURSE*	Poori (deep-fried bread)
		Bagara khana (fried spicy rice)
		Jhingay aur saag (prawns with spinach)
		Tamatar ki chutney (tomato curry)
		Tarka dhaal (oil-dressed dhaal)
	DESSERT	Badaam ka halva (almond dessert)
MENU 3	*MAIN COURSE*	Poori (deep-fried bread)
		Saag panir (spinach cheese)
		Masala vale aloo (spicy potatoes)
		Tarka dhaal (oil-dressed dhaal)
	DESSERT	Sooji ka halva (semolina dessert)

MENU 4 *MAIN COURSE*   Chapati (unleavened bread)
Khushka (plain boiled rice)
Sookhay jhingay (dried prawns)
Dahi ki kadi (dumplings in a yoghurt sauce)
Thurai aur methi (courgettes with fresh fennel leaves)

DESSERT   Badaam ka halva (almond dessert)

MENU 5 *MAIN COURSE*   Poori (deep-fried bread)
Pulao (rice cooked with saffron and cardamoms, etc.)
Masalay dar aloo phalli (spicy potato and green beans)
Dahi vale baingun (fried aubergines in yoghurt)
Pakoray (deep-fried vegetable dumplings)
Khadi dhaal (onion dhaal)

DESSERT   Sooji ka halva (semolina dessert)

MENU 6 *MAIN COURSE*   Masala dosa (stuffed rice pancakes with a potato filling and chutney)
(This one dish makes a simple snack or supper on its own.)

MENU 7 *MAIN COURSE*   Poori (deep-fried bread)
Khushka (plain boiled rice)
Aloo gobi (potato and cauliflower curry)
Bengali machli (Bengali-style fish)
Khatti dhaal (lemon dhaal)

DESSERT   Chawal ki kheer (rice pudding)

MENU 8 *MAIN COURSE*   Parata (layered bread)
Khushka (plain boiled rice)
Kabli chana bhujia (chick pea curry)
Besun may thali huwi machli (fried fish in gram flour)
Tarka dhaal (oil-dressed dhaal)

DESSERT   Firni (ground rice pudding)

Brunch

Though for everyday breakfasts we like to eat similar foods to those eaten in the West, Indians like to have something different at weekends and holidays, especially if we have people staying with us or joining us for Sunday brunch. *Nehari* (meat cooked in spices and herbs, in a thick sauce) is a great favourite; ideally this should be cooked all night and served hot with *naans* or *paratas*, but what I do is cook it the previous afternoon to serve, heated up, the next morning – it is a great standby for after a New Year's Eve party, or when we have guests spending a weekend with us. Served as a late breakfast, it is very filling and keeps everyone satisfied for a long time afterwards, so there is no need for lunch. In India you can buy *nehari* ready cooked to bring home, and when I was a child one of my uncles used to get up early to fetch the *nehari* at weekends; everyone at home would wait hungrily for his return with this popular 'take-away'.

In the north of India people like to eat the potato dish *aloo bhujia*, the sweet semolina dessert known as *sooji ka halva*, and *pooris* – deep-fried, puffed-up breads. All these are fairly quick and easy to prepare.

Among the other dishes I particularly enjoy at either breakfast or brunch are fried kidneys, stir-fried cauliflower and *badaam ka hareera* (a dessert made with ground almonds and milk). You can accompany these either with a fried egg or with an Indian-style omelette (page 127) and *paratas* – or just ordinary toasted bread.

The traditional breakfast drink is Indian tea, but for brunch you may wish to serve lager or beer, fruit juice or other soft drinks.

MENU 1   Khageena (egg curry)
Parata (layered bread)
Lassi (yoghurt drink)
Aam ki chutney (mango chutney)

MENU 2   Thalay huway gurday (fried kidneys)
Parata (layered bread)
Tarka dhaal (oil-dressed dhaal)
Lime pickle

DESSERT
Badaam ka hareera (ground almonds cooked in ghee and milk)

MENU 3   Roghni roti (lightly fried bread)
Indian-style omelette
Aam ki chutney (mango chutney)
Thali huwi phool gobi (fried cauliflower)

MENU 4   Kheema matar (minced lamb with peas)
Parata (layered bread)
Lime pickle
Lassi (yoghurt drink)

MENU 5   Nehari (hot, spicy lamb in sauce)
Naan (yeasted bread)
Lassi (yoghurt drink)

MENU 6   Poori (deep-fried bread)
Aloo bhujia (potato curry)
Aam ki chutney (mango chutney)
Lime pickle

DESSERT
Sooji ka halva (semolina dessert)

MENU 7   Shaami kebabs (meat kebabs)
Poori (deep-fried bread)
Fried eggs
Lime pickle

CHAPTER 3

Preparation and Cookery Tips

Now that you have confirmed your guest list and planned your menu, the next step is to make a list of the items you need to buy. Check your stocks of spices, lentils and rice, in particular, so that you do not end up duplicating items you already have – or, far worse, discover halfway through cooking that your stock of a certain commodity is virtually gone (see section on store-cupboard items below).

After you have done the shopping and are ready to start on the meal itself, check through your recipes quickly to be sure you know what sort of timing is required for each dish, and work out in advance which, if any, you are going to freeze until needed.

For an important meal, I find it helpful to make notes to remind me to attend to the details which might otherwise get overlooked, such as taking something out of the freezer, making a salad or pre-heating the oven. Last-minute decoration such as fresh coriander or green chilli should also be prepared and left in a prominent place so that it does not get forgotten, preferably covered with clingwrap to prevent drying out. Doing this can save a great deal of unnecessary tension and panic.

It is also a good idea, particularly if you are not already familiar with Indian cooking, to measure out all the spices you need before you start cooking and keep them either on a plate or in small separate bowls. Chop the onions and any other vegetables, too.

EQUIPMENT FOR INDIAN COOKING
Your own kitchen will probably be equipped already with everything needed for cooking a full range of Indian dishes. Some good-quality saucepans, with thick bases, and a heavy-bottomed frying-pan will take you a long way, and you will want some wooden spatulas and, ideally, a slotted spoon for stirring rice, to use with them. You will want at least one good, sharp knife and for measuring some spoons and a jug. Kitchen scales could be helpful, too.

For grinding spices you can use a pestle and mortar, a coffee grinder or food processor, or a rolling-pin: in many Indian households a flat, heavy grindstone and something like a rolling-pin (called a *mussal*) are still considered the best solution. Some people find a garlic press useful, too, for Indian cookery.

In an Indian kitchen you would probably find a *thawa*, which is a cast-iron frying-pan used for cooking chapatis and paratas and for roasting spices; a *karahi*, a deep-frying pan which resembles a straight-sided wok, made of aluminium or stainless steel, with handles on both sides; and possibly also a *girda*, a small (25 cm/10 inches in diameter) pastry board on short legs, used for rolling out dough. However, many people now use a clean kitchen worktop for rolling out. You might also find an electric rice cooker helpful. These have become popular throughout the East wherever rice is cooked regularly and in large quantities, because they ensure the rice is always perfectly cooked, will keep it warm until required – and prevent a good many burnt saucepans, too, no doubt.

If you have a pressure cooker you might well find it useful for Indian cooking: it will certainly reduce the cooking time for large joints of lamb or beef. If using either a pressure cooker or a slow cooker, you must brown the onions first and stir-fry the meat and spices briefly before setting it (this will greatly improve both flavour and colour), and be sure to cook the food until the surplus liquid has been absorbed. In the case of a pressure cooker, you can remove the lid for this final stage. You will also find a pressure cooker useful for *dhaals*, some of which (depending, very often, on how long they have been on the shelf in the shop) can take a long time to tenderize.

For entertaining, a freezer is invaluable. If I am preparing a big dinner, I usually start preparing about a week to ten days in advance (two or three days before is ample for a small gathering) and freeze the dishes as I make them. All the kebabs in this book, and the majority of the curries, freeze beautifully, whether meat or vegetarian. There is one vegetable, however, that becomes mushy when cooked and frozen: potato. So when you cook a dish that includes potato with the intention of freezing, leave out the potato and add it on the day you are going to serve it.

To re-heat on the day, either place the item in the oven, in a saucepan or under a low grill depending on the item concerned; you could also shallow-fry, but I find this makes the dishes a little greasy. A microwave oven is of course the latest answer to thawing and re-heating frozen dishes, but check carefully how much time you will need to cope with all the different items as a microwave's capacity is limited.

Finally, do not forget that if you have a hostess trolley this too can come into its own when you entertain Indian-style. It will enable you to keep all the dishes hot until the moment you put them on the table, and even give you time, if you wish, to clear up the kitchen and wash up the pots and pans before your guests arrive. It will also give you a more relaxed evening because it will save you darting backwards and forwards to the kitchen.

STORE-CUPBOARD ITEMS

Your basic stock of spices should include fresh ginger and garlic, chilli powder, turmeric, cardamom, black pepper, ground coriander and cumin. The powdered spices will keep very well in airtight containers, carefully labelled, while the fresh ginger and garlic will keep for seven to ten days in the refrigerator. Other useful items, to be acquired as your repertoire increases, are cumin seeds (black as well as white), onion seeds, mustard seeds, cloves, cinnamon, dried red chillis, fenugreek, vegetable ghee and garam masala (a mixture of spices that can either be bought ready-made or home-made in quantity for use whenever required: see recipe on page 30). Tomato purée is also useful to have at hand.

USING SPICES

There are many ways of using spices. You can use them whole, ground, roasted, fried or mixed with yoghurt to marinate meat and poultry. One spice can completely alter the flavour of a dish and a combination of several can produce a different colour and texture.

The quantities of spices shown in the recipes in this book are merely a guide. Do not hesitate to increase or decrease these as you wish, especially in the cases of salt and chilli powder, which are very much a matter of taste. Remember that long cooking over a lowish heat will always improve the taste of the food as it allows the spices to be absorbed. This is why re-heating the following day is no problem in the case of most Indian food. Do feel free to experiment with the different spices, and above all, taste everything: only you know how you want your food to taste.

Many of the recipes in this book call for ground spices, which are generally available in supermarkets as well as in Indian and Pakistani grocers. In India we almost always buy whole spices and grind them ourselves, and there is no doubt that freshly ground spices do make a noticeable difference to the taste. However, there is no denying that it is more convenient, and quicker, to use ground spices.

For some of the recipes, the spices need to be roasted. In India this is done on a *thawa*, but failing this utensil you can use a heavy, ideally cast-iron, frying-pan. No water or oil is added to the spices: they are simply dry-roasted whole while the pan is shaken to stop them burning.

GINGER AND GARLIC PULP

As ginger and garlic are used very frequently in curries, and it takes time and effort to peel and chop these every time, I suggest you take about 200 g (8 oz) of each, soak them overnight (this makes them easy to peel), peel and grind them – separately, in a food processor, adding a little water to form a pulp. They can then be stored in an airtight container in a cool place for a month or even longer.

YOGHURT

When adding yoghurt to curries I always whip it first with a fork so that it does not curdle, and I add it gradually. Yoghurt helps to tenderize the meat and give curry a thick, creamy texture. Always use natural unsweetened yoghurt. *Raita*, yoghurt sauce, complements most curries beautifully.

THE SECRET OF A GOOD CURRY

The final colour and texture of a curry depend on how well you browned the onions in the first stage. This requires patience, especially if you are cooking a large quantity. Heat the oil first, before you add the onions, then reduce the heat slightly so that the onions go golden brown without burning, and stir them gently with a wooden spoon or spatula.

Once this is done, add the spices, meat or other ingredients, as stipulated in the recipe, and mix and coat the meat by 'bhoono-ing' (stirring and frying in semi-circular movements, scraping the bottom of the pan). This is essential for a good end-result, and when you have done this you should taste the food and adjust the seasoning according to your own palate. Remember, my recipes are only guidelines, not prescriptions, so you do not have to follow them too rigidly.

THICKENING SAUCES

In Indian cooking flour is very seldom used to thicken sauces; instead, we rely upon the onions and on spices such as ginger, garlic or powdered coriander to produce a thick brown sauce.

MAKING A BAGHAAR (SEASONED OIL DRESSING)

This dressing is quite unique and as far as I know is used only in Indian cooking. The oil or ghee is heated to a very high temperature without burning, the spices, onions and herbs are dropped into the oil, immediately changing colour and becoming very aromatic; then the seasoned oil is removed from the heat and poured over the dish – cooked *dhaals* or vegetables, very often – like a dressing. Sometimes uncooked food is added to the heated oil, too, to be sautéd or simmered.

You will find full instructions for *baghaars* in the recipes, wherever they are required: for example, on page 42, cauliflower with meat.

PRESENTATION

There are few 'rules' about presenting Indian food, but if you are entertaining have in mind which containers you will use for each dish and try not to neglect the final decorative touches – the fresh coriander leaves, or the chopped chilli – that make the food look as appetizing as it tastes.

Curries and *dhaals* (lentils) are served in large, deep dishes, rice is piled on flat, oval-shaped dishes and *raita* (yoghurt sauce) is best served in a sauce boat. Breads, such as *chapatis*, *paratas* or *pooris*, should be served on a plate wrapped in foil to keep them warm as long as possible. Pickles, chutneys and *kachoomer* (onions and tomatoes in lemon juice) are eaten in small portions so it is best to put these in small bowls, each with a teaspoon in them, so that people do not take large helpings (in any case, some of the pickles can be very hot and are certainly not intended to be eaten on their own).

Guests usually help themselves from the serving dishes. Rice is placed in the centre of the dinner plate, leaving some room for the curries, which are never put on top of the rice. It is not necessary to help yourself to everything that is placed on the table at once.

Though you will probably wish to provide a cruet set for the dinner table, it is a mistake for anyone to add salt before tasting because it has always been added with all the other spices during cooking.

Decoration for the food, such as coriander leaves and green chilli, is best if fresh, but both of these items can be kept frozen in polythene bags or small freezer containers for convenience. Do not wash the coriander before freezing it; just rinse it under a cold tap before use. Coriander is fairly easy to grow in the back garden, especially during the summer months, and I have been reasonably successful growing it on the windowsill – so it is worth a try for this sometimes difficult-to-find herb. Other garnishes, especially for kebabs or dry chicken pieces, include onion rings, tomatoes and lemon wedges, which are both attractive and inexpensive.

By contrast, a rather special way of decorating both savoury dishes and desserts is to use *varq* (beaten silver leaf, which is edible). This method of decoration probably started with the Moghuls, perhaps seeking to intrigue their guests at palace banquets, and is reserved for very special occasions because it is quite an expensive item. A dessert decorated with *varq* certainly looks very beautiful, and is bound to impress your guests. It also provides quite a talking point. However, it is real silver, so it may not be very pleasant for anyone with fillings in their teeth.

The table itself can be graced with a central floral arrangement – ideally, not a very high one, because this will get in everyone's way and be a nuisance when people are trying to converse across the table. When fresh flowers are few and far between, the highly realistic silk arrangements now on sale are very effective – and more economical in the long run, too, if you do not have a garden from which to gather flowers.

As for cutlery, there is perhaps nothing better than traditional silver, which has been used in India for a very long time, especially for more formal occasions. In family or less formal situations, however, it is still common for people to eat with the fingers of the right hand (considered the cleaner of the two), after both hands have been washed scrupulously.

Finally, if you want to clear your home of cooking smells before your guests arrive, try lighting up a few incense sticks (*agar battis*) about an hour before the guests are due. I find these are far better than any air fresheners you can buy, and they come in various fragrances including jasmine and rose.

CHAPTER 4
Glossary

Aamchoor Mango powder made from dried raw mangoes. It has a sour taste and can be bought in jars.
Ata Wholemeal flour, *q.v.*

Bay leaf (*tez patta*) One of the oldest herbs used in cookery, although not very widely used in curries.
Besun Gram flour, *q.v.*
Bhoonay chanay Dried roasted chick peas, bought in packets.

Cardamom (*elaichi*) This spice, native to India, is considered the second most expensive (after saffron). The pods can be used with or without their husks and have a slightly pungent but very aromatic taste. They come in three varieties: green, white and black. The green and white pods can be used for both sweet and savoury dishes or to flavour rice, the black only for savoury dishes.
Cayenne pepper *See* chilli powder.
Chana dhaal Very similar in appearance to moong dhaal – the yellow split peas – this lentil has slightly less shiny grains. It is used as a binding agent for kebabs and other dishes and may be bought from Indian or Pakistani grocers.
Chana dhaal flour Gram flour, *q.v.*
Chapati flour *See* wholemeal flour.
Chilli powder (*laal mirch*) or cayenne pepper. A very fiery spice that should be used with caution.
Chillis, dried red (*sabath sookhi laal mirch*). These pods are extremely fiery and should be used with caution; their effect can be toned down slightly by removal of the seeds. Dried chillis are usually fried in oil before use.
Chillis, fresh green (*hari mirch*). Beautifully aromatic in flavour, these are used both in cooking and as a decoration. The seeds, which are the hottest part, may be removed if desired, by splitting the chilli down the middle. Never touch the face, especially the eyes, while or after handling chillis: even after washing your hands will sting. Chillis are grown in Africa and Indonesia.
Cinnamon (*dhalchini*) One of the earliest known spices, this is grown mainly in Sri Lanka and has an aromatic and sweet flavour. It is sold both in powdered form and as sticks.
Cloves (*laung*) This spice is used to flavour many sweet and savoury dishes and is usually added whole. It is also sometimes used to seal a betel leaf for serving after an Indian meal (see *paan*).
Coconut (*khopra* or *narial*) Used to flavour both sweet and savoury dishes, fresh coconut can often be bought in supermarkets. Desiccated coconut and creamed coconut can also be bought and for most dishes make acceptable substitutes. Coconut is sometimes toasted for use in dishes (as for spices, see pages 26–7).
Coriander, fresh (*hara dhania*) This beautifully fragrant herb is used both in cooking and, finely chopped, sprinkled over dishes as a garnish.
Coriander seeds (*dhania*) This aromatic spice has a pungent, slightly lemony flavour. The seeds are used widely, either coarsely ground or powdered, in meat, fish and poultry

dishes. The ground seeds, a brownish powder, are an important constituent of any mixture of curry spices.

Corn oil Less fattening than any of the other oils, especially ghee, and also free from smell, this is my preferred type of cooking oil.

Cumin (*safaid zeera*) This musty-smelling ground spice is used widely, especially for flavouring lentils and vegetable curries. Its flavour improves upon roasting or frying.

Cumin seeds (*shah zeera*) Black cumin seeds, which have a strong aromatic flavour, are used to flavour curries and rice. White cumin may not be used as a substitute.

Curry leaves (*kari patta*) Similar in appearance to bay leaves but very different in flavour, these can be bought both fresh (occasionally) and dried. They are used to flavour lentil dishes and vegetable curries.

Fennel seeds (*sonfe*) Very similar-looking to white cumin, these have a very sweet taste and are used to flavour certain curries. They can also be chewed (as betelnut and cardamom are) after a spicy meal.

Fenugreek (*methi*) The flavour of the whole, dried, flat yellow seeds, a little bitter in taste, improves when they are lightly fried. Fresh fenugreek, sold in bunches, has very small leaves and is used to flavour both meat and vegetarian dishes.

Garam masala This is a mixture of spices which can either be made up at home from freshly ground spices or bought ready-made. There is no set formula, but a typical mixture might include black cumin seeds, peppercorns, cloves, cinnamon and black cardamom. To make your own, grind together 4 2.5-cm (1-inch) cinnamon sticks, 3 cloves, 3 black peppercorns, 2 black cardamoms (with husks removed) and 10 ml (2 teaspoons) black cumin seeds. If desired, multiply the quantities, grind, and store in an airtight jar for future use.

Garlic (*lassun*) This very useful spice is frequently used in curries, especially with ginger. It can be puréed in large quantities in a food processor and kept in an airtight container in the refrigerator. Whole cloves are sometimes added to lentil dishes.

Ghee (clarified butter) There are two types: pure (a dairy product) and vegetable. Though it was once a matter of pride to be able to claim that everything served in one's household was cooked in pure ghee, pure ghee is in fact quite high in cholesterol, so from the health standpoint it is better to use vegetable ghee or vegetable oil wherever possible (the majority of curries are cooked in oil). To make up your own pure ghee melt 300 g (8 oz) in a heavy saucepan and allow to simmer for 10–20 minutes. Once the white milky froth has begun to turn golden, strain (preferably through muslin or cheesecloth) and store in a jar.

Ginger root (*adrak*) One of the most popular spices in India and also one of the oldest, this is an important ingredient in many curries and can be bought in good supermarkets. It should always be peeled before use and can be puréed in a food processor. Dried powdered ginger (*sontt*) is also useful to have in your larder.

Gram flour (*besun*) or chana dhaal flour (lentil flour) is used to make *pakoras* and is also used to bind kebabs and other items. A combination of gram flour and ordinary wholemeal flour makes a delicious Indian bread called *besun ki roti*.

Kevra water Iris water, used to flavour sweet dishes and sometimes rice. It is sold in small bottles.

Masoor dhaal Small, round and pale orange, in colour, these split lentils become pale yellow in colour when cooked. All supermarkets stock them, usually labelled simply 'lentils'.

Moong dhaal This is a tear-drop-shaped yellow split lentil, more popular in northern India than in the south.

Mustard oil This is often used in Bengali dishes, especially for cooking fish.

Mustard seeds (*sarson ke beenj*) (*rai*) These seeds, either black or yellow, are round in shape and sharp in flavour. They are used for flavouring curries and pickles.

Nutmeg (*jaifal*) The flavour of nutmeg, a native of Indonesia, is sweet and aromatic.

Onion seeds (*kalongi*) Black in colour and triangular in shape, these are used for both pickles and vegetable curries.

Paan Betel leaf dressed with calcium paste, fennel seeds, cardamom seeds, etc., wrapped and held together with a clove and sometimes covered with *varq* (edible silver leaf), for serving at the end of the evening to guests at an Indian party. It acts as a mouth-freshener and coats the mouth with a red colouring. It can be bought or made at home, and may or may not contain tobacco. *Paan* can however be addictive if it contains tobacco.

Paprika This powder, made from dried sweet red pepper, is known as a hot-flavoured spice but is nothing like as hot as chilli pepper. Paprika is not used very often in Indian cookery.

Pepper Whenever possible use freshly ground black pepper if an Indian recipe stipulates pepper.

Pistachio nuts Widely used in Indian desserts, these are not the salty type sold in their shells but the shelled ones sold in packets at all Indian and Pakistani grocers.

Poppy seeds (*khush khush*) These dried whole seeds are always better when toasted. They are used, often whole, to flavour curries. Although they are from the opium poppy, they do not contain opium.

Rose water This is used mainly to flavour certain sweetmeats.

Saffron (*zafran*) This, the world's most expensive spice, is made from the stigmas of the saffron crocus, which is native to Asia Minor. Each 500 g (1 lb) saffron needs 60,000 stigmas. Fortunately only a small quantity of saffron is needed to flavour or colour a dish, whether sweet or savoury. Saffron is sold both as strands and in powder form. It has a beautiful flavour and fragrance.

Sesame seeds (*thill*) Whole, flat, cream-coloured seeds, these are used to flavour some curries. When ground, they can be made into chutney.

Sev These are very thin sticks made of gram flour which can be bought in Indian and Pakistani grocers.

Tamarind (*imli*) The dried black pods of the tamarind plant, also known as the Indian date, are sour in taste and very sticky. Tamarind has to be soaked in hot water to extract the flavour. Though it is much stronger than lemon, lemon is often used as a substitute. Nowadays tamarind can be bought in paste form in jars: mix with a little water to bring it to a runny consistency. Tamarind grows freely in India.

Turmeric (*haldi*) This bright yellow, bitter-tasting spice is sold ground. It is used mainly for colour rather than flavour.

Urid dhaal Though very similar in shape and size to moong dhaal, this dhaal is white and a little drier when cooked. It is popular amongst northern Indians.

Urid dhaal flour This very fine white flour is used for *vadas* (deep-fried dumplings) which when soaked in yoghurt make a delicious light snack, and for *dosas* (Indian rice pancakes).

Varq Edible beaten silver leaf used for decoration purposes. It should be handled gently as it is very light and airy. It can be bought in sheets from Indian or Pakistani grocers, but you may have to order it.

Wholemeal flour (*ata*) Also known as chapati flour, this may be bought at any Indian or Pakistani grocers' shop. It is used to make chapatis, *paratas* and *pooris*. Ordinary wholemeal flour may also be used for Indian breads, very well sieved.

Opposite Raan *(roast lamb and* masalay vale aloo *(spicy potatoes), with peas and corn.*

Overleaf *A special dinner-party menu, with lamb biryani,* paratas, murgh makhani *(buttered chicken),* aloo gobi *(potato and cauliflower),* chahni huwi dhaal aur kofteh *(dhaal with meatballs),* masalay dar corn *(spicy corn), cucumber salad and a dessert of carrot halva and fresh fruit.*

THE RECIPES

For all recipes, quantities are given in both metric and imperial measures. Follow either but do not mix the two, because they are not interchangeable. All spoon measurements in this book are level.

Titles of recipes are in most cases given in Urdu as well as English, and occasionally I use certain Urdu cookery terms such as *bhoono* and *baghaar* for convenience. The following checklist of such words will enable you to see at a glance what they mean.

aam mango
aamchoor Mango powder
achaar Pickle
akhrot Walnut
aloo Potato
anda Egg
angoor Grape

badaam Almond
badi mirch Green pepper
baghaar Seasoned oil dressing
baingun Aubergine
besun Gram flour
bhoono To stir-fry using semi-circular movements, scraping the bottom of the pan
bhajia Dumpling
bhujia Vegetable curry
bhindi Okra (lady's fingers)
boti Boned meat
bund gobi Cabbage

chapati Unleavened bread
chawal Rice
chukander Beetroot

dahi Yoghurt
dhaal Lentils
dhania Coriander
dum Oven-cooked in its own juices

gajar Carrot
goshth Meat

halva Sweet, dessert
hara dhania Fresh green coriander
hari mirch Green chillis

jhinga Prawn

kaddu Pumpkin
kaju Cashew nut
kela Banana
khatti Sour

kheema Minced meat
kheera Cucumber
khorma Yoghurt-based curry
khushka Plain boiled rice
kish-mish Raisins

lassi Yoghurt-based drink

machli Fish
makhan Butter
masala Spice
matar Peas
mooli White radish
murgh Chicken

naan Yeasted bread
neembu Lemon

palak Spinach
parata Layered bread
phool gobi Cauliflower
piaz Onions
podina Mint
poori Puffed-up, deep-fried bread

raita Yoghurt-based sauce
roti Bread

saag Spinach
sabath Whole
salan Curry
seb Apples
shakar kand Sweet potato
shorwa Sauce, gravy, of curry
sooji Semolina
sookhay Dry
subzee Vegetable

tamatar Tomato
thalan Fried

vada Dumpling

zafran Saffron

CHAPTER 5
Meat (goshth)

There is a wide variety of meat recipes in this book, and in most cases the meat is lamb. I prefer to use leg of lamb, as it is much less fatty than shoulder, but if you like shoulder I suggest you combine it with an equal proportion of leg, which works very well.

In some of the recipes beef (braising steak, for example) may be substituted for lamb, but if you do this you will need to allow a little extra cooking time.

Most of my recipes call for meat on the bone; if you prefer, take the meat off the bone before you cook it.

Masalay vale chops
SPICY LAMB CHOPS

This is an attractive way of serving chops, especially if you garnish them with potato chips, tomatoes and lemon wedges. Serve these with any *dhaal* and rice or chapati.

SERVES 4–6
1 kg (2 lb) lamb chops
10 ml (2 teaspoons) fresh ginger, pulped
10 ml (2 teaspoons) fresh garlic, pulped
5 ml (1 teaspoon) ground black pepper
5 ml (1 teaspoon) garam masala
5 ml (1 teaspoon) black cumin seeds
7.5 ml (1½ teaspoons) salt
900 ml (1½ pints) water
2 medium eggs
300 ml (½ pint) oil
potato chips, tomatoes and lemon wedges to garnish

Remove all the fat from the chops. Add all the spices to the chops and boil in the water for about 45 minutes, stirring occasionally. Once the water has evaporated remove from the heat and set aside to cool. Beat the eggs in a large bowl. Heat the oil in a saucepan, dip each chop into the egg and fry in the oil for 3 minutes, turning once. Arrange the chops on a large dish and garnish with fried potato chips, tomato and lemon wedges. Serve hot.

Aamchoor ka dopiaza
LAMB WITH ONIONS & DRIED MANGO POWDER

This dish originates from Hyderabad, in central southern India.

SERVES 4
4 medium onions
300 ml (½ pint) oil
5 ml (1 teaspoon) fresh ginger, pulped
5 ml (1 teaspoon) fresh garlic, pulped
5 ml (1 teaspoon) chilli powder
1 pinch turmeric
5 ml (1 teaspoon) salt
3 green chillis
450 g (1 lb) leg of lamb, cubed
600 ml (1 pint) water
7.5 ml (1½ teaspoons) aamchoor *(dried mango powder)*
fresh coriander

Chop 3 onions finely. Heat 150 ml (¼ pint) of the oil and fry until golden brown. Lower the heat and add all the spices except the *aamchoor*. Stir-fry for about 5 minutes. Add 2 green chillis. Add the meat and stir-fry (using the *bhoono*-ing method) for a further 7 minutes. Add the water, cover and cook over a low heat for 35–45 minutes, stirring occasionally. Meanwhile slice the remaining onion, heat the remaining oil in a saucepan and fry until golden brown. Leave aside. Check to see whether the meat is tender and add the *aamchoor*, the green chilli and fresh coriander leaves. Stir-fry for 3–5 minutes. Transfer the curry into a serving dish and pour the fried onion and oil along the centre. Serve hot.

Pasandeh
SLICED LAMB COOKED WITH YOGHURT & SPICES

There are many different ways of cooking *pasandeh*, but this is my particular favourite. However, for this recipe you need to roast the spices, as this helps give the dish a nice dark colour and a richer taste. Serve with *chapati* and white lentils.

SERVES 4
2 medium onions
450 g (1 lb) lean lamb slices, cut into 2.5-cm
(1-inch) slices
75 ml (5 tablespoons) yoghurt
5 ml (1 teaspoon) fresh ginger, pulped
5 ml (1 teaspoon) fresh garlic, pulped
5 ml (1 teaspoon) chilli powder
1 pinch turmeric
10 ml (2 teaspoons) garam masala
5 ml (1 teaspoon) salt
2 cardamoms
5 ml (1 teaspoon) black cumin seeds
50 g (2 oz) ground almonds
300 ml ($\frac{1}{2}$ pint) oil
15 ml (1 tablespoon) desiccated coconut
15 ml (1 tablespoon) poppy seeds
15 ml (1 tablespoon) sesame seeds
300 ml ($\frac{1}{2}$ pint) water
2 green chillis
a few fresh coriander leaves, chopped

Chop the onions finely and leave aside. In a separate bowl mix the lamb with the yoghurt, ginger, garlic, chilli powder, turmeric, garam masala, salt, cardamoms and black cumin seeds and set aside.

Roast the ground almonds, desiccated coconut, poppy seeds and sesame seeds until golden brown (see pages 26–7). Grind in a food processor until fine and well mixed together. Add 15 ml (1 tablespoon) water to blend if necessary. Add this mixture to the meat and mix together.

In a large saucepan heat a little oil and fry the chopped onions until golden brown. Remove the onions from the pan. Stir-fry the meat in the oil remaining for about 5 minutes, then return the onions to the pan and stir-fry (using the *bhoono*-ing method) for 5–7 minutes. Add the water and simmer over a low heat, covered, for 25–30 minutes, stirring occasionally. Add the green chillis and coriander leaves.

Note Substitute beef for lamb in this recipe if desired.

Tamatar ka khorma
TOMATO COOKED WITH MEAT & YOGHURT

One of my favourites, this delicious tomato *khorma* has a semi-thick sauce. I like to serve freshly made *chapatis* with it.

SERVES 2–4
5 ml (1 teaspoon) garam masala
5 ml (1 teaspoon) fresh ginger, pulped
5 ml (1 teaspoon) fresh garlic, pulped
2 black cardamoms
5 ml (1 teaspoon) chilli powder
2.5 ml (½ teaspoon) black cumin seeds
2 2.5-cm (2 1-inch) cinnamon sticks
5 ml (1 teaspoon) salt
150 ml (5 fl oz) natural yoghurt
½ kg (1 lb) lean cubed lamb
150 ml (¼ pint) oil
2 medium onions, sliced
600 ml (1 pint) water
2 firm tomatoes
30 ml (2 tablespoons) lemon juice
GARNISH
   fresh coriander leaves, chopped
   2 green chillis, chopped

In a large mixing bowl combine all the spices, the yoghurt and the meat and mix well. Leave aside.

Heat up the oil in a large saucepan and fry the onions until golden brown. Add the meat to the onions and stir-fry (using the *bhoono*-ing method) for about 5 minutes. Lower the heat, add the water, cover and simmer for about 1 hour, stirring occasionally. Cut the tomatoes into quarters and drop these into the curry; sprinkle with lemon juice and simmer for a further 7–10 minutes.

Garnish with the fresh coriander leaves and the chopped green chillis.

Roghan goshth
LAMB CURRY IN A THICK SAUCE

Originally a Kashmiri dish, this lamb stew is now made all over India and is popular wherever Indian food is eaten. Noted for its delicious tomato-flavoured sauce, it is ideal for a dinner party.

SERVES 6
1 kg (2 lb) lean lamb, cubed, with or without bone
105 ml (7 tablespoons) yoghurt
75 g (3 oz) almonds
10 ml (2 teaspoons) garam masala
10 ml (2 teaspoons) fresh ginger, pulped
10 ml (2 teaspoons) fresh garlic, pulped
7.5 ml (1½ teaspoons) chilli powder
7.5 ml (1½ teaspoons) salt
300 ml (½ pint) oil
3 medium onions, finely chopped
4 green cardamoms
2 bay leaves
3 green chillis, chopped
30 ml (2 tablespoons) lemon juice
400-g (14-oz) can tomatoes
300 ml (½ pint) water
coriander leaves, chopped

Combine the cubed lamb, yoghurt, almonds, garam masala, ginger, garlic, chilli powder and salt. Heat the oil in a large saucepan and fry the onions with the cardamoms and the bay leaves until golden brown. Add the meat and yoghurt mixture and stir-fry for 3–5 minutes. Add two green chillis, the lemon juice and the canned tomatoes. Stir-fry for a further 5 minutes. Add the water and leave to simmer over a low heat for 35–40 minutes. Add the remaining green chilli and the fresh coriander leaves and stir occasionally until the sauce has thickened. Remove the lid and turn the heat higher if the sauce is too watery.

Kheema matar
MINCED LAMB WITH PEAS

Served with a *dhaal* and rice, this simple dish makes a well-balanced meal.

SERVES 4
1 medium onion
90 ml (6 tablespoons) oil
3 green chillis, chopped
coriander leaves
2 tomatoes, chopped
5 ml (1 teaspoon) salt
5 ml (1 teaspoon) fresh ginger, pulped
5 ml (1 teaspoon) fresh garlic, pulped
5 ml (1 teaspoon) chilli powder
500 g (1 lb) lean minced lamb
100 g (4 oz) peas

Peel and slice the onion. In a medium-sized saucepan heat the oil and fry the onions until golden brown. Add two green chillis, half of the fresh coriander and the chopped tomatoes. Lower the heat. Add the spices and blend in. Add the mince and stir-fry for 7–10 minutes (using the *bhoono*-ing method). Put the peas in and stir for a further 3–4 minutes.

Garnish with the remaining green chilli and the fresh coriander leaves.

Gurday
KIDNEYS

Many people are resistant to the idea of cooking or eating kidneys because they often have rather a strong smell – even when cooked. But if you wash and soak them you can largely avoid this. All you have to do is to remove the very fine skin, cut each kidney into 4–6 pieces and soak these in warm water with 10 ml (2 teaspoons) turmeric and 10 ml (2 teaspoons) salt for about 1 hour. Drain, then wash the pieces under the cold tap until the water runs clear. Then follow the recipe.

Thalay huway gurday
FRIED KIDNEYS

Fried lamb kidneys are a popular dish for a late breakfast or brunch, served with *paratas* and a fried egg.

SERVES 4
500 g (1 lb) lamb kidneys
1 green pepper
150 ml ($\frac{1}{4}$ pint) water
5 ml (1 teaspoon) fresh ginger, pulped
5 ml (1 teaspoon) fresh garlic, pulped
5 ml (1 teaspoon) chilli powder
2.5 ml ($\frac{1}{2}$ teaspoon) salt
45 ml (3 tablespoons) oil
1 small onion, chopped
coriander leaves to garnish

Prepare the kidneys according to the instructions above and wash thoroughly. Place with the green pepper in a small saucepan, cover with water and cook over a medium heat, leaving the lid so that steam can escape, until the water has evaporated. Blend in all the spices, then the oil, the finely chopped onion and the fresh coriander leaves, and stir-fry for 7–10 minutes. Serve hot.

Shorway vale kheema kay kofteh
MEATBALLS IN SAUCE

This is an old family recipe. The *koftas* (meatballs) are easy to make and also freeze beautifully.

SERVES 4
450 g (1 lb) minced lamb
5 ml (1 teaspoon) fresh ginger, pulped
5 ml (1 teaspoon) fresh garlic, pulped
5 ml (1 teaspoon) garam masala
7.5 ml (1½ teaspoons) poppy seeds
5 ml (1 teaspoon) salt
2.5 ml (½ teaspoon) chilli powder
1 medium onion, finely chopped
1 green chilli, finely chopped
coriander leaves
15 ml (1 tablespoon) ground bhoonay chanay
  (roasted dry chick peas)
SAUCE
  150 ml (¼ pint) oil
  3 medium onions, finely chopped
  2 small cinnamon sticks
  2 large black cardamoms
  5 ml (1 teaspoon) chilli powder
  5 ml (1 teaspoon) ground coriander
  1 pinch turmeric
  5 ml (1 teaspoon) fresh ginger, pulped
  5 ml (1 teaspoon) fresh garlic, pulped
  5 ml (1 teaspoon) salt
  75 ml (3 fl oz) natural yoghurt
  150 ml (¼ pint) water
  coriander leaves
  1 green chilli

Place the mince in a mixing bowl and add all the spices, including the finely chopped onion, green chilli and coriander leaves and ground *bhoonay chanay*, mix well with a fork and make small balls with the palm of the hand. Leave aside.

Heat the oil, fry the finely chopped onions until golden brown. Add the cinnamon and the black cardamoms. Lower the heat and stir-fry for a further 5 minutes. Add all the other spices, the salt and the natural yoghurt and stir to mix well. Gently drop the *koftas* one by one into this and add the water. Stir, gently turning the *koftas* once, and cook over a low heat for 25–30 minutes. Decorate with finely chopped coriander leaves and green chilli.

Serve with *chapatis*.

Goshth aur phool gobi
CAULIFLOWER WITH MEAT

I love vegetables cooked with meat, especially cauliflower and spinach, which have a lovely flavour cooked this way. For this recipe I use only a few spices but I like to add a *baghaar* (a seasoned oil dressing) at the end. You can have either *chapati* or plain boiled rice with this and I think tomato curry (*tamatar ki chutney*) also goes very well.

SERVES 4
2 onions
1 medium cauliflower
coriander leaves
2 green chillis
300 ml ($\frac{1}{2}$ pint) oil
450 g (1 lb) cubed lamb, with bone
7.5 ml (1$\frac{1}{2}$ teaspoons) fresh ginger, pulped
7.5 ml (1$\frac{1}{2}$ teaspoons) fresh garlic, pulped
5 ml (1 teaspoon) chilli powder
5 ml (1 teaspoon) salt
900 ml (1$\frac{1}{2}$ pints) water
15 ml (1 tablespoon) lemon juice
BAGHAAR
    150 ml ($\frac{1}{4}$ pint) oil
    4 dried red chillis
    5 ml (1 teaspoon) mixed mustard and onion seeds

Peel and slice the onion. Cut the cauliflower into very small florets. Chop the fresh coriander and green chillis. Heat 300 ml ($\frac{1}{2}$ pint) oil in a large saucepan and fry the onions until golden brown. Lower the heat and add the meat, ginger, garlic, chilli powder and salt, blend and stir-fry for about 5 minutes. Add 1 green chilli and half of the coriander leaves. Stir in the water and cook covered over a low heat for about 30 minutes. Add the cauliflower and simmer for a further 15—20 minutes or until the water has evaporated completely. Stir-fry (using the *bhoono-ing* method) for another 5 minutes. Turn the heat off. Sprinkle over the lemon juice sparingly.

In a separate small saucepan heat the remaining oil and fry the dried red chillis and the mixed mustard and onion seeds until they turn darker. Remove from the heat and pour over the cooked cauliflower.

Garnish with the remaining green chilli and coriander leaves.

Nargisi kofteh
MEAT-COATED EGGS

These koftas are ideal for taking on a picnic, because they are dry. In fact, they are more or less the Indian equivalent of the scotch egg. However, if you wish to serve these in a sauce use the one in the recipe for *kofta* curry.

SERVES 6
1 small onion
1 green chilli
500 g (1 lb) lean minced lamb
5 ml (1 teaspoon) fresh ginger, pulped
5 ml (1 teaspoon) fresh garlic, pulped
5 ml (1 teaspoon) ground coriander
5 ml (1 teaspoon) garam masala
5 ml (1 teaspoon) salt
20 ml (1½ tablespoons) gram flour
7 eggs, 6 of them hard-boiled and shelled, 1 beaten
oil for deep frying

Finely chop the onion and the green chilli.

In a separate bowl blend together the minced lamb, finely chopped onion and the green chilli, then grind these in a food processor. Remove from the processor and add all the spices, gram flour and the beaten egg. Combine together using your hand. Divide the mixture into 6 equal portions. Roll each portion out flat, place a hard-boiled egg in the middle of each and enclose the egg in the meat mixture, about 5 mm (¼ inch) thick. When all 6 eggs have been covered, leave in a cool place for 20–30 minutes.

Meanwhile, heat the oil in a *karahi* or a deep-frying pan, gently drop the *koftas* into the oil and fry for 2–4 minutes or until golden brown, moving them carefully with a perforated spoon. Remove the *koftas* from the pan and drain on kitchen paper.

Nehari
HOT, SPICY LAMB IN SAUCE

This is a very hot and spicy curry with a thick sauce – a typical North Indian dish that is traditionally served for a late breakfast or brunch. Ideally it should be cooked all night and served in the morning with *naans*, but otherwise it can be cooked the previous day and re-heated.

SERVES 6–8
15 ml (1 tablespoon) ground garam masala
10 ml (2 teaspoons) fresh ginger, pulped
10 ml (2 teaspoons) fresh garlic, pulped
7.5 ml (1½ teaspoons) salt
10 ml (2 teaspoons) chilli powder
15 ml (1 tablespoon) ground coriander
10 ml (2 teaspoons) ground nutmeg
15 ml (1 tablespoon) ground fennel seeds
15 ml (1 tablespoon) paprika
5 medium onions
170 ml (6 fl oz) oil
1 kg (2 lb) lean leg of lamb, cut into large pieces
150 ml (5 fl oz) yoghurt
30 ml (2 tablespoons) tomato purée
900 ml (1½ pints) water
15 ml (1 tablespoon) bhoonay chanay *or gram flour*
3 bay leaves
15 ml (1 tablespoon) plain flour
GARNISH
    4–6 green chillis, chopped
    fresh coriander leaves, chopped
    fresh ginger, peeled and shredded
    1 lemon, cut into wedges
    1 small onion, sliced

Measure and prepare all the spices. Chop the onions finely.

Heat the oil, add the meat and half of the garam masala, stir-fry and coat the meat well. Continue frying for 7–10 minutes. Using a slotted spoon remove all the meat and place in a bowl. Add the chopped onions and fry until golden brown. Place the meat back in the saucepan. Stir and lower the heat.

In a separate bowl mix together the yoghurt and tomato purée, ginger, garlic, salt, chilli powder, ground coriander, nutmeg and the rest of the garam masala. Pour this mixture over the meat and stir-fry (using the *bhoono*-ing method), mixing the spices well into the meat, for 5–7 minutes. Add half of the water, then the ground fennel, paprika and ground *bhoonay chanay*. Add the remaining water, drop the bay leaves in, lower the heat, cover and cook for 1 hour, stirring occasionally. Mix the plain flour in about 30 ml (2 tablespoons) warm water and pour over the *nehari*. Sprinkle over half of the green chillis and fresh coriander and cook until the meat is tender and the sauce thickens.

Serve hot with the prepared garnish and *naan* or *paratas*.

Badaami khorma
LAMB KHORMA WITH ALMONDS

This *khorma*, a traditional northern Indian recipe, has a thick sauce and is quite simple to cook.

SERVES 6
300 ml ($\frac{1}{2}$ pint) oil
3 medium onions
1 kg (2 lb) lean lamb, cubed, with or without bone
7.5 ml (1$\frac{1}{2}$ teaspoons) garam masala
7.5 ml (1$\frac{1}{2}$ teaspoons) ground coriander
7.5 ml (1$\frac{1}{2}$ teaspoons) fresh ginger, pulped
7.5 ml (1$\frac{1}{2}$ teaspoons) fresh garlic, pulped
5 ml (1 teaspoon) salt
150 ml (5 fl oz) natural yoghurt
2 cloves
3 green cardamoms
4 black peppercorns
600 ml (1 pint) water
GARNISH
   6 almonds, soaked, peeled and chopped
   2 green chillis, chopped
   a few coriander leaves

Heat the oil in a saucepan. Add the finely chopped onions and stir-fry until golden brown. Remove half the onions from the pan and leave aside. Add the meat to the remaining onions and stir-fry for about 5 minutes. Remove from the heat. In a separate bowl mix all the ground spices with the yoghurt and gradually add to the meat. Return the saucepan to the heat, and stir for 5–7 minutes, or until the mixture is nearly brown in colour. Add the cloves, whole cardamoms and whole black peppercorns. Add the water and lower the heat, cover and simmer for about 45–60 minutes. If the water has completely evaporated but the meat is not tender enough, add another 300 ml ($\frac{1}{2}$ pint) water and cook for a further 10–15 minutes, stirring occasionally. Before serving, add the remaining onions, almonds, green chillis and the fresh coriander leaves.

   Serve with *chapati*.

Note Substitute beef for lamb in this recipe if desired.

Aloo ka khorma
POTATOES COOKED WITH MEAT & YOGHURT

Khormas almost always contain yoghurt and therefore have lovely, smooth sauces. A good accompaniment would be *chapati*, or *bagara khana* with peas.

SERVES 6
3 medium onions
3 medium potatoes
300 ml ($\frac{1}{2}$ pint) oil
1 kg (2 lb) leg of lamb, cubed, with or without bone
5 ml (2 teaspoons) garam masala
7.5 ml (1$\frac{1}{2}$ teaspoons) fresh ginger, pulped
7.5 ml (1$\frac{1}{2}$ teaspoons) fresh garlic, pulped
5 ml (1 teaspoon) chilli powder
3 black peppercorns
3 green cardamoms
5 ml (1 teaspoon) black cumin seeds
2 cinnamon sticks
5 ml (1 teaspoon) paprika
7.5 ml (1$\frac{1}{2}$ teaspoons) salt
150 ml (5 fl oz) natural yoghurt
600 ml (1 pint) water
GARNISH
   2 green chillis
   chopped coriander leaves

Peel and slice the onions and leave aside. Peel and cut the potatoes into sixes. Heat the oil in a saucepan and fry the sliced onions until golden brown. Remove the onions from the pan. Add the meat to the saucepan with 5 ml (1 teaspoon) of the garam masala and stir-fry for 5–7 minutes over a low heat. Add the onions to the meat and turn the heat off.

In a small bowl mix all the spices (ground as well as whole) with the yoghurt. Turn the heat on again and gradually add the spice and yoghurt mixture to the meat and onions and stir-fry for 7–10 minutes (using the *bhoono*-ing method). Add the water, lower the heat and cook, covered, for about 40 minutes, stirring occasionally. Put the potatoes in and cook, covered, for a further 15 minutes, gently stirring from time to time.

Garnish with green chillis and fresh coriander leaves.

Maya khalia
SPICY LAMB CURRY IN SAUCE

This curry is especially good served with plain boiled rice and *khadi* (onion) *dhaal*. Traditionally tamarind is used for this recipe but I like to use lemon juice.

SERVES 4

10 ml (2 teaspoons) ground cumin
10 ml (2 teaspoons) ground coriander
10 ml (2 teaspoons) desiccated coconut
5 ml (1 teaspoon) mixed mustard and onion seeds
10 ml (2 teaspoons) sesame seeds
5 ml (1 teaspoon) fresh ginger, pulped
5 ml (1 teaspoon) fresh garlic, pulped
5 ml (1 teaspoon) chilli powder
5 ml (1 teaspoon) salt
500 g (1 lb) lean lamb
450 ml ($\frac{3}{4}$ pint) oil
3 medium onions, sliced
900 ml (1$\frac{1}{2}$ pints) water
30 ml (2 tablespoons) lemon juice
4 green chillis, split

Roast (see pages 26–7) and grind the cumin, coriander, desiccated coconut, mixed mustard and onion seeds and the sesame seeds. In a large mixing bowl blend together the roasted ground spices along with the other spices and cubed lamb and leave aside.

In a separate saucepan heat up 300 ml ($\frac{1}{2}$ pint) of the oil and fry the sliced onions until golden brown. Add the meat mixture and stir-fry for 5–7 minutes on a low heat. Add the water and simmer for 45 minutes, stirring occasionally. When the meat is cooked, remove from the heat and sprinkle over the lemon juice.

In a separate saucepan, heat up the remaining oil and add the four split green chillis. Lower the heat and cover with a lid. Remove from the heat after about 30 seconds and leave to cool. Pour this over the meat curry and serve hot with *khadi dhaal* (page 88) and plain boiled rice.

Sabath masala goshth
LAMB COOKED IN WHOLE SPICES

SERVES 4
3 medium onions
300 ml (½ pint) oil
2.5 cm (1 inch) shredded ginger
4 cloves shredded garlic
2 cinnamon sticks
3 whole green cardamoms
3 whole cloves
4 whole black peppercorns
6 dried red chillis
150 ml (5 fl oz) yoghurt
500 g (1 lb) lamb, with or without bone
3 green chillis, chopped
600 ml (1 pint) water
fresh coriander leaves

Chop the onion finely and fry in the oil until golden brown. Lower the heat and add all the whole spices. Stir-fry for 5 minutes. Whip the yoghurt with a fork and add to the onions. Blend everything together. Add the meat and 2 green chillis. Stir-fry (using the *bhoono*-ing method) for 5–7 minutes. Add the water gradually and cover and cook for 1 hour, stirring occasionally. Add more water if necessary. When cooked, remove from the heat and transfer to a serving dish.

Garnish with the remaining chopped green chilli and fresh coriander leaves.

Note Substitute beef for lamb in this recipe if desired.

Raan
LAMB POT ROAST

I have always found this to be a great success at dinner parties, when I usually serve it with vegetable rice and masala potatoes (*masala vale aloo*).

SERVES 6
2.5 kg (5 lb) leg of lamb, with the fat removed
10 ml (2 teaspoons) fresh ginger, pulped
10 ml (2 teaspoons) fresh garlic, pulped
10 ml (2 teaspoons) garam masala
5 ml (1 teaspoon) salt
10 ml (2 teaspoons) black cumin seeds
4 black peppercorns
3 cloves
5 ml (1 teaspoon) chilli powder
45 ml (3 tablespoons) lemon juice
300 ml ($\frac{1}{2}$ pint) oil
1 large onion, peeled
2 litres (4 pints) water

Prick the leg of lamb with a fork. Blend all the spices together with the lemon juice and rub all over the leg of lamb. Put the oil in the saucepan. Place the meat in the saucepan and put the whole onion on the side of the leg. Cover with sufficient water and cook over a low heat for $2\frac{1}{2}$–3 hours. Check occasionally. If the water has evaporated and the meat is not tender add a little extra water. Once the water has dried up, move the roast around with a spoon to brown it all over. Remove from the pan and serve either sliced or whole, to be carved at the table. This dish may be served hot or cold.

Saag goshth
LEAN LAMB COOKED IN SPINACH

I like to serve this nutritious combination with plain boiled rice and tomato curry (*tamatar ki chutney*).

SERVES 2–4
2 medium onions
300 ml (½ pint) oil
¼ bunch fresh coriander
3 green chillis, chopped
7.5 ml (1½ teaspoons) fresh ginger, pulped
7.5 ml (1½ teaspoons) fresh garlic, pulped
5 ml (1 teaspoon) chilli powder
2.5 ml (½ teaspoon) turmeric
500 g (1 lb) lean lamb, with or without bone
5 ml (1 teaspoon) salt
1 kg (2 lb) fresh spinach, trimmed, washed and
   chopped, or 425 g (15 oz) canned spinach
750 ml (1¼ pints) water
GARNISH
   shredded ginger
   fresh coriander

Peel and slice the onions, heat the oil in a saucepan and fry the onions until they turn pale. Add the fresh coriander and 2 chopped green chillis and stir-fry for 3–5 minutes. Turn the heat low, add all the spices and blend well. Put the lamb in and stir-fry for a further 5 minutes. Add the salt and fresh or canned spinach and stir. Mix, preferably with a wooden spoon, for a further 3–5 minutes (using the *bhoono*-ing method). Stir in the water and cook over a low heat with the lid on for about 45 minutes. Remove the lid and check the meat. If it is not tender, turn, increase the heat and cook uncovered until the surplus water has been absorbed. Stir-fry (using the *bhoono*-ing method) for 5–7 minutes. Remove from the heat and transfer to a serving dish. Garnish with shredded ginger, fresh coriander leaves and the remaining chopped green chilli.

Khichra
LAMB COOKED WITH FOUR TYPES OF LENTIL

In this recipe I use four different types of lentils and porridge oats. This takes some time to cook as you have to cook the lamb *khorma* separately. But *khichra* is a meal in itself so you do not need to make *chapati* or rice. Once the *khorma* is cooked and the lentils are boiled and mashed they are mixed and given a *baghaar* (seasoned oil dressing). Served garnished with green chillis, coriander leaves, shredded ginger and lemon wedges, the dish makes a well balanced meal on its own. It is also good for dinner parties.

SERVES 6
100g (4oz) chana dhaal
100g (4oz) masoor dhaal
100g (4oz) moong dhaal
100g (4oz) urid dhaal
75g (3oz) porridge oats
KHORMA
  1.5kg (3lb) lamb, cubed with bones
  200ml (7fl oz) yoghurt
  10ml (2 teaspoons) fresh ginger, pulped
  10ml (2 teaspoons) fresh garlic, pulped
  15ml (1 tablespoon) garam masala
  10ml (2 teaspoons) chilli powder
  2.5ml ($\frac{1}{2}$ teaspoon) turmeric
  3 whole green cardamoms
  2 cinnamon sticks
  5ml (1 teaspoon) black cumin seeds
  10ml (2 teaspoons) salt
  5 medium onions
  450ml ($\frac{3}{4}$ pint) oil
  750ml (1$\frac{1}{4}$ pints) water
  2 green chillis
  coriander leaves
GARNISH
  6 green chillis, chopped
  $\frac{1}{2}$ bunch coriander leaves, chopped
  2 pieces fresh ginger, shredded
  3 lemons, cut into wedges

Pick over the *dhaals* carefully, wash and soak with the porridge oats overnight. Boil together in a large saucepan until soft enough to mash, mash and leave aside.

Place the lamb in a large bowl. Stir the yoghurt in, add all the spices and salt, mix and leave aside. Peel and slice four of the onions. Heat 300ml ($\frac{1}{2}$ pint) oil in a large saucepan and fry the sliced onions until golden brown. Add the meat to the onions and stir-fry (using the *bhoono*-ing method) for 7–10 minutes. Gradually stir in the water, lower the heat and cook covered for 1 hour, stirring occasionally. Check the meat: if it is not tender add more water and cook for a further 15–20 minutes. Turn the heat off. Add the mashed lentils to the meat *khorma*, stir and mix well. If the mixture is too thick add 300ml ($\frac{1}{2}$ pint) water, stir and cook for 10–12 minutes.

Add the two green chillis and the chopped coriander leaves. Transfer to a serving dish and leave this aside. In a frying-pan heat the remaining oil and fry the onions until a crisp golden brown. Pour the *baghaar* over the *khichra*. Serve hot, garnished with green chillis, fresh coriander leaves, shredded ginger and lemon wedges.

Kheema bhare tamatar
STUFFED TOMATOES

This is an impressive dinner-party dish. You will find large tomatoes are easier to fill. Note that the same recipe may be used for green or red peppers.

SERVES 4–6
6 large, firm tomatoes
50g (2oz) unsalted butter
1 medium onion, peeled and finely chopped
75ml (5 tablespoons) oil
5ml (1 teaspoon) fresh ginger, pulped
5ml (1 teaspoon) fresh garlic, pulped
5ml (1 teaspoon) ground black pepper
5ml (1 teaspoon) salt
2.5ml ($\frac{1}{2}$ teaspoon) garam masala
500g (1lb) minced lamb
1 green chilli
fresh coriander leaves

Wash the tomatoes, cut off the tops and de-seed. Grease a heatproof dish with 50g (2oz) butter, and place the tomatoes on it. Peel and finely chop the onion, heat the oil in a saucepan and fry the onion until golden brown. Lower the heat and add the ginger, garlic, ground black pepper, salt and garam masala. Stir-fry for 3–5 minutes. Add the mince and fry for 10–15 minutes. Add the green chilli and fresh coriander leaves and continue stir-frying for a further 3–5 minutes. Spoon the *kheema* into the tomatoes and cover with the tops. Heat the oven to 180°C, 350°F, Gas 4 and place the tomatoes in the oven for 15–20 minutes. Remove from the oven and serve hot.

CHAPTER 6

Vegetarian Dishes

A great many people in India are vegetarians – possibly the majority. The reasons for this are mainly religious, so over the years Indians have used their imaginations to create a vast variety of different vegetarian dishes, among them *aloo gobi* (cauliflower and potato), *bhindi bhujia* (okra), chick pea and other vegetarian curries, and the many *dhaal*, or lentil, dishes.

Today, many non-vegetarians are beginning to include vegetarian dishes in their menus and to eat the occasional meatless meal, especially since the health pundits began to warn us of the dangers of cholesterol and encourage us to cut down on red meat, in particular, for the good of our health.

Spinach, tomatoes, potatoes, green beans and cauliflower are all commonly used in Indian cooking, but some popular Indian vegetables, including aubergines, okra (sometimes known as lady's fingers) and mooli, or white radish, are less familiar in the West despite the fact that they are now widely available. In the section that follows I have included some simple but delicious vegetarian dishes using these vegetables – some in a sauce, some dry – that will help to familiarize you with them.

In strict vegetarian households neither fish nor even eggs are included in the diet, which means it lacks protein (and certain vitamins). This is why it is important to serve a *dhaal* as part of a vegetarian meal – all lentils are packed with protein. A *raita* (yoghurt sauce) makes an excellent accompaniment to any vegetarian meal, and for carbohydrate I think the best choice is plain boiled rice or, alternatively, *pooris* (deep-fried bread puffs).

In India, vegetarian meals are traditionally served in *thalis* – small stainless steel bowls on a stainless steel tray.

Dahi ki kadi
DUMPLINGS IN A YOGHURT SAUCE

I use gram flour to flavour and thicken the sauce in this recipe, and add a *baghaar* (seasoned oil dressing) just before serving. It makes a mouth-watering accompaniment to any meal and can be prepared in advance. This dish need not be served warm.

SERVES 4
BHAJIAS
    100g (4oz) gram flour
    5ml (1 teaspoon) chilli powder
    2.5ml (½ teaspoon) salt
    2.5ml (½ teaspoon) bicarbonate of soda
    1 medium onion, chopped
    2 green chillis
    fresh coriander leaves
    150ml (¼ pint) water
    300ml (½ pint) oil
KADI
    300ml (10fl oz) yoghurt
    45ml (3 tablespoons) gram flour
    150ml (¼ pint) water
    5ml (1 teaspoon) fresh ginger, pulped
    5ml (1 teaspoon) fresh garlic, pulped
    7.5ml (1½ teaspoons) chilli powder
    7.5ml (1½ teaspoons) salt
    2.5ml (½ teaspoon) turmeric
    5ml (1 teaspoon) ground coriander
    5ml (1 teaspoon) ground cumin
BAGHAAR
    150ml (¼ pint) oil
    5ml (1 teaspoon) white cumin seeds
    6 red dried chillis

Sieve the gram flour, add the chilli powder, salt, soda, finely chopped onion, green chillis and fresh coriander leaves and mix together. Add the water to form a thick paste. Heat the oil in a frying-pan. Using a teaspoon, drop the gram flour gently into the oil and fry, turning once, over a medium heat until a crisp golden brown. Leave the *bhajias* (dumplings) aside.

In a large bowl whisk the yoghurt with the gram flour and the water, add all the spices and mix well. Put this mixture through a large sieve into a saucepan. Place the saucepan over a low heat and bring to the boil, stirring continuously. If the *kadi* (curry) becomes too thick add a little extra water. Remove from the heat. Transfer to a deep serving dish and add all the *bhajias*.

Prepare the *baghaar* by heating the oil in a frying-pan. Add the white cumin seeds and the dried red chillis, fry until darker in colour and pour this over the *kadi* in the bowl.

Saag panir
SPINACH CHEESE

This vegetarian curry is full of protein and iron. Serve as a side dish with meat curries or as part of a vegetarian menu. *Panir* is a type of cheese.

SERVES 4
300 ml ($\frac{1}{2}$ pint) oil
200 g (8 oz) panir, cubed (see below)
3 tomatoes, sliced
5 ml (1 teaspoon) ground cumin
7.5 ml (1$\frac{1}{2}$ teaspoons) ground coriander
7.5 ml (1$\frac{1}{2}$ teaspoons) chilli powder
5 ml (1 teaspoon) salt
400 g (15 oz) spinach
3 green chillis

Heat the oil in a saucepan and fry the cubed *panir* until golden brown. Remove from the pan and leave to drain on kitchen paper. Add the sliced tomatoes to the remaining oil and stir-fry, breaking up the tomatoes, for 5 minutes. Mix all the spices in and then add the spinach. Stir-fry over a low heat for 7–10 minutes. Add the green chillis. Finally, add the *panir* and cook for a further 2 minutes. Serve hot with *pooris* or plain boiled rice.

Note To make *panir*, boil 1 litre (1$\frac{3}{4}$ pints) milk slowly over a low heat, then add 30 ml (2 tablespoons) lemon juice, stirring continuously and gently until the milk thickens and begins to curdle. Strain the curdled milk through a sieve. Set aside under a heavy weight for about 1$\frac{1}{2}$–2 hours to press to a flat shape about 1 cm ($\frac{1}{2}$ inch) thick. Once set, the *panir* can be cut, like cheese, into whatever shape is required.

Mooli bhujia
WHITE RADISH CURRY

This is rather an unusual recipe for a vegetarian curry. The vegetable used is mooli, or white radish, which looks a bit like a parsnip without the tapering end and is now sold in supermarkets as well as in Indian and Pakistani grocers. The dish is good served hot with *chapati*.

SERVES 4
500 g (1 lb) mooli (preferably with leaves)
15 ml (1 tablespoon) moong dhaal
600 ml (1 pint) water
1 medium onion
150 ml ($\frac{1}{4}$ pint) oil
5 ml (1 teaspoon) fresh garlic
5 ml (1 teaspoon) crushed red chillis
5 ml (1 teaspoon) salt

Wash, peel and roughly slice the mooli with its leaves. Boil these in the water together with the moong dhaal until the mooli is soft enough to be squeezed by hand. Drain and squeeze out any excess water, using your hands. Slice the onion thinly. Heat the oil in a saucepan and fry the sliced onion, garlic, crushed red chillis and salt. Stir the mooli mixture into the onion and combine well. Lower the heat and continue stirring gently for about 3–5 minutes.

Aloo bhujia
POTATO CURRY

Served hot with *pooris, aloo bhujia* makes an excellent brunch with mango chutney as an accompaniment. Traditionally semolina halva (*sooji ka halva*) is served at the same meal.

SERVES 4
3 medium potatoes
15 ml ($\frac{1}{4}$ pint) oil
5 ml (1 teaspoon) onion seeds
2.5 ml ($\frac{1}{2}$ teaspoon) fennel seeds
4 curry leaves
5 ml (1 teaspoon) ground cumin
5 ml (1 teaspoon) ground coriander
5 ml (1 teaspoon) chilli powder
1 pinch turmeric
5 ml (1 teaspoon) salt
7.5 ml (1$\frac{1}{2}$ teaspoons) aamchoor (dried mango powder)

Peel, wash and cut the potatoes into six cakes each. Boil the potatoes until just cooked – not mushy (test by piercing with a sharp knife or a skewer).

  In a separate saucepan heat the oil, then lower the heat and start adding the spices: first the onion and fennel seeds, then the curry leaves. Remove from the heat and add all the ground spices. Return to the heat and stir-fry for about 1 minute. Pour this mixture, or *baghaar*, over the cooked potatoes, mix together and stir-fry for about 5 minutes on a low heat.

Thali huwi phool gobi
FRIED CAULIFLOWER

A dry dish flavoured with a few herbs, this is a very versatile accompaniment.

SERVES 4
60 ml (4 tablespoons) oil
2.5 ml (½ teaspoon) onion seeds
2.5 ml (½ teaspoon) mustard seeds
2.5 ml (½ teaspoon) fenugreek seeds
4 dried red chillis
1 small cauliflower, cut into small florets
5 ml (1 teaspoon) salt
1 green pepper, diced

Heat the oil in a saucepan. Add all the seeds and the dried red chillis. Lower the heat. Gradually add all the cauliflower and salt. Stir-fry for 7–10 minutes. Add the diced green pepper. Stir-fry for a further 3–5 minutes. Serve hot.

Khageena
EGG CURRY

This curry can be made very quickly. It can either be served as a side dish or, with *paratas*, at breakfast or brunch.

SERVES 4
1 medium onion, sliced
1 green chilli
1 firm tomato
60 ml (4 tablespoons) oil
2.5 ml (½ teaspoon) chilli powder
2.5 ml (½ teaspoon) fresh ginger, pulped
2.5 ml (½ teaspoon) fresh garlic, pulped
4 medium eggs
fresh coriander leaves

Peel and slice the onion. Chop the green chilli. Slice the tomato. Heat the oil in a saucepan, fry the sliced onion until soft; add the green chilli and the spices and stir-fry, over a lower heat, for about 1 minute. Add the eggs and sliced tomato and continue stirring for 3–5 minutes, breaking up the eggs when they begin to cook. Sprinkle over the fresh coriander leaves and serve hot with *paratas*.

Subzee ke kebab
VEGETABLE KEBABS

If you invite several people to dinner or to a buffet meal nowadays there is a strong chance that one of them may be a vegetarian. So I always try to make at least one vegetarian dish, and what better than a vegetarian kebab? These are quick and easy to make and can be prepared in advance. They are also a good way of persuading children to eat vegetables, as well as making a welcome change from vegetable curry.

MAKES 10–12
2 large potatoes
1 medium onion
½ medium cauliflower
50 g (2 oz) peas
15 ml (1 tablespoon) spinach purée
2–3 green chillis
fresh coriander
5 ml (1 teaspoon) fresh ginger, pulped
5 ml (1 teaspoon) fresh garlic, pulped
5 ml (1 teaspoon) ground coriander
1 pinch turmeric
5 ml (1 teaspoon) salt
50 g (2 oz) breadcrumbs
300 ml (½ pint) oil

Peel and slice the potatoes and onion and cut the cauliflower. Boil these vegetables together until the potatoes are well cooked, and drain. Add the peas and spinach to the vegetables and mix together, mashing down with a fork.

Finely chop the green chillis and fresh coriander and mix this with all the other spices. Blend into the vegetables and mix with a fork.

Break off small balls to make flat, round shapes in the palm of your hand, then dip each kebab in the fine breadcrumbs. Heat the oil in a heavy frying-pan and shallow-fry until golden brown.

Khatti sookhi bhindi
DRY SPLIT OKRA

This is an unusual way of cooking this delicious vegetable. The dish is dry when cooked, and should be served hot with chapati and *dhaal.*

SERVES 4
500g (1 lb) okra
150 ml (¼ pint) oil
100 g (4 oz) dried onions
10 ml (2 teaspoons) aamchoor *(dried mango powder)*
5 ml (1 teaspoon) ground cumin
5 ml (1 teaspoon) chilli powder
5 ml (1 teaspoon) salt

Prepare the okra by cutting both the ends off and discarding, then splitting the okra down the middle without cutting through completely.

In a saucepan, heat the oil and lightly fry the dried onions until crisp. Turn off the heat and remove the onions on to kitchen paper with a slotted spoon. When cool, break up with your hands. Add all the spices and the salt and blend well together.

Fill the split okra with this mixture. Re-heat the oil in the saucepan and gently drop the okra into it. Cook over a low heat for about 10–12 minutes.

Bhindi bhujia
OKRA CURRY

This is a delicious dry *bhujia* (vegetarian curry) which should be served hot with *chapati.* As okra is such a tasty vegetable it does not need many spices.

SERVES 4
500g (1 lb) okra
1 tomato
150 ml (¼ pint) oil
2 medium onions
3 green chillis
2 curry leaves
5 ml (1 teaspoon) salt
30 ml (2 tablespoons) lemon juice
coriander leaves

Wash the okra. Chop and discard the ends of the okra and cut into 2.5-cm (1-inch)-long pieces.

Slice the tomato. Slice the onions and chop the green chillis. In a large, heavy frying-pan heat the oil and add the sliced onions, chopped green chillis, curry leaves and salt. Combine all ingredients together. Stir-fry for 5 minutes. Gradually add the okra, mixing in gently with a slotted spoon. Stir-fry over a medium heat for 12–15 minutes. Add the sliced tomato and sprinkle over the lemon juice sparingly.

Decorate with coriander leaves, cover and simmer for 3–5 minutes.

Tamatar ki chutney
TOMATO CURRY

Though this curry is called a chutney it is simply a vegetarian tomato curry which is cooked without onions. Served topped with a few hard-boiled eggs it makes a lovely accompaniment to almost any meal, and goes particularly well with *kitcheri* (page 104). It also freezes well.

SERVES 4
400 g (15 oz) canned tomatoes
5 ml (1 teaspoon) fresh ginger, pulped
5 ml (1 teaspoon) fresh garlic, pulped
5 ml (1 teaspoon) chilli powder
5 ml (1 teaspoon) salt
2.5 ml (½ teaspoon) ground coriander
2.5 ml (½ teaspoon) ground cumin
60 ml (4 tablespoons) oil
2.5 ml (½ teaspoon) onion seeds
2.5 ml (½ teaspoon) mustard seeds
2.5 ml (½ teaspoon) fenugreek seeds
1 pinch white cumin seeds
3 dried red chillis
30 ml (2 tablespoons) lemon juice
3 eggs, hard-boiled
coriander leaves

Place the tomatoes in a bowl. Add the ginger, garlic, chilli powder, salt, ground coriander and ground cumin and blend well. In a separate saucepan heat the oil and add the onion, mustard, fenugreek and white cumin seeds, and the dried red chillis, and stir-fry for about 1 minute. Remove from the heat and place the saucepan on a draining board.

Add the tomato mixture to the oil and return to the heat. Stir-fry for about 3 minutes, lower the heat and cook with the lid ajar for 7–10 minutes, stirring occasionally. Sprinkle over the lemon juice sparingly. Remove from the heat and transfer to a serving dish.

Shell and halve the hard-boiled eggs, then gently drop them, yolk end down, into the curry. Garnish with fresh coriander leaves. Serve hot.

Kaddu curry
PUMPKIN CURRY

The Indian pumpkin used in this curry is long and green and sold by weight. It can easily be bought from any Indian or Pakistani grocers. This curry is best served with freshly made *besun ki roti* (gram flour bread).

SERVES 4
150 ml (¼ pint) oil
2 medium-sized onions
2.5 ml (½ teaspoon) white cumin seeds
500 g (1 lb) green pumpkin, cubed
5 ml (1 teaspoon) aamchoor (dried mango powder)
5 ml (1 teaspoon) fresh ginger, pulped
5 ml (1 teaspoon) fresh garlic, pulped
5 ml (1 teaspoon) crushed red chilli
2.5 ml (½ teaspoon) salt
300 ml (½ pint) water

Heat the oil and fry the onions with the cumin seeds. Add the cubed pumpkin and stir-fry for 3–5 minutes over a low heat.

Blend all the spices together and add to the onion mixture. Add 300 ml (½ pint) water, cover and cook over a low heat for 10–15 minutes, stirring occasionally.

Masalay dar aloo phalli
GREEN BEANS & POTATO CURRY

You can use fresh or canned green beans for this semi-dry vegetable curry. I would recommend you serve a *tarka dhaal* (page 91) with this, for a good contrast of flavours and colours.

SERVES 4
300 ml (½ pint oil
5 ml (1 teaspoon) white cumin seeds
5 ml (1 teaspoon) mustard and onion seeds
4 dried red chillis
3 fresh tomatoes, sliced
5 ml (1 teaspoon) salt
5 ml (1 teaspoon) fresh ginger, pulped
5 ml (1 teaspoon) fresh garlic, pulped
5 ml (1 teaspoon) chilli powder
200 g (8 oz) green cut beans
2 medium potatoes, peeled and diced
300 ml (½ pint) water
fresh coriander, chopped
2 green chillis

Heat the oil in a saucepan and fry the white cumin seeds, mustard and onion seeds and dried red chillis. Add the sliced tomatoes and stir-fry for 3–5 minutes. Blend in the salt, ginger, garlic and chilli powder. Add the green beans and potatoes. Stir-fry for about 5 minutes. Add the water, lower the heat and simmer for 10–15 minutes, stirring occasionally. Garnish with chopped coriander and green chillis.

Masala vale aloo
POTATOES WITH SPICES & ONIONS

Masala aloo are potatoes cooked in spices and onions. Semi-dry when cooked, they make an excellent accompaniment to almost any meat or vegetable curry. You could also serve these, for a change, with roast lamb or lamb chops.

SERVES 4
2 medium-sized onions
5 ml (1 teaspoon) fresh ginger, pulped
5 ml (1 teaspoon) fresh garlic, pulped
5 ml (1 teaspoon) chilli powder
5 ml (1 teaspoon) salt
7.5 ml (1½ teaspoons) ground cumin
7.5 ml (1½ teaspoons) ground coriander
350-g (14-oz) can new potatoes
15 ml (1 tablespoon) lemon juice
90 ml (6 tablespoons) oil
BAGHAAR
   45 ml (3 tablespoons) oil
   3 dried red chillis
   2.5 ml (½ teaspoon) onion seeds
   2.5 ml (½ teaspoon) mustard seeds
   2.5 ml (½ teaspoon) fenugreek seeds
fresh coriander leaves
1 green chilli

Chop the onions very finely (use a food processor if available) and fry until golden brown. Lower the heat, add all the spices and salt and stir-fry for about 1 minute. Remove from the heat and set aside. Drain the water from the potatoes and add these to the onion mixture. Sprinkle over the lemon juice and mix well.

In a separate saucepan heat the oil and add all the *baghaar* ingredients. Fry until the seeds turn a shade darker. Remove from heat and pour the *baghaar* over the potatoes.

Garnish with fresh coriander leaves and chopped green chillis.

Kabli chana bhujia
CHICK PEA CURRY

This is very popular amongst vegetarian people in India. There are many different ways of cooking chick peas. I use canned chick peas because this saves time, but if you use dried chick peas soak them overnight then boil them for 15–20 minutes until soft.

SERVES 4
90 ml (6 tablespoons) oil
2 medium onions
5 ml (1 teaspoon) fresh ginger, pulped
5 ml (1 teaspoon) ground cumin
5 ml (1 teaspoon) ground coriander
5 ml (1 teaspoon) fresh garlic, pulped
5 ml (1 teaspoon) chilli powder
2 green chillis
fresh coriander leaves
150 ml ($\frac{1}{4}$ pint) water
1 large potato
400 g (14 oz) canned chick peas
15 ml (1 tablespoon) lemon juice

Heat the oil in a saucepan. Fry the sliced onions until golden brown. Lower the heat and start adding all the spices, the green chillis and fresh coriander leaves. Stir-fry for 2 minutes. Add the water. Peel and dice the potato and add this along with the drained can of chick peas, cover and simmer for 5–7 minutes. Sprinkle over the lemon juice. Turn off the heat. Serve with *chapati*.

Opposite *This spread is for a formal dinner party, showing chicken tikka and* naan *(yeasted bread), which could be served together as a starter, and* dum ka kheema *(grilled minced lamb),* tamatar jhingay *(prawn tomato curry), cucumber* raita, *carrot and mint salad,* pulao *rice and a dessert of* shahi tukray *(Indian bread pudding).*

Overleaf, left *The stuffed* poori, *or bread puffs, with their filling shown separately on the terracotta plate, and the* chawal ki kheer *(rice pudding) topped with* varq *represent a special meal that Muslims cook for the festival of Koonday (see page 141).*

Overleaf, right *This vegetarian brunch, served on a traditional* thali — *the stainless steel tray and dishes — features* bagara khana *(fried spicy rice),* poori *(deep-fried bread puffs),* aloo bhujia *(potato curry), lime pickle and* sooji ka halva *(a dessert made with semolina). The stainless steel dishes always signify a vegetarian meal to Indians.*

Aloo gobi
POTATO & CAULIFLOWER CURRY

Potatoes and cauliflower go very well together. Served with a *dhaal* and *pooris*, this dish makes a perfect vegetarian meal.

SERVES 4
150 ml (¼ pint) oil
2.5 ml (½ teaspoon) white cumin seeds
4 dried red chillis
2 medium onion, sliced
5 ml (1 teaspoon) fresh ginger, pulped
5 ml (1 teaspoon) fresh garlic, pulped
5 ml (1 teaspoon) chilli powder
5 ml (1 teaspoon) salt
1 pinch turmeric
3 medium potatoes
¼ cauliflower, cut into small florets
2 green chillis (optional)
fresh coriander leaves
150 ml (¼ pint) water

Wash and prepare all the vegetables.

Heat the oil in a saucepan, add the white cumin seeds and dried red chillis. Add the onions and fry until golden brown. Mix all the spices and add to the onions. Stir-fry for about 2 minutes. Add the potatoes and cauliflower to the onion mixture and lower the heat. Add the green chillis, fresh coriander leaves and water, cover and simmer for 10–15 minutes.

Opposite *Another brunch menu, this time with* thalay huway gurday *(fried kidneys),* roghni roti *(gram-flour bread), an Indian-style omelette and mango chutney, with an almond pudding* (badaam ka hareera) *to follow.*

Bagaray baingun
AUBERGINES COOKED IN PICKLING SPICES

This is a very versatile dish that will go with almost anything and can be served warm or cold. It will keep in the refrigerator for 3–5 days, and also freezes very well. It is excellent served with a few hard-boiled eggs, and perhaps with boiled rice, and it is also very good with a biryani and *shaami* kebabs. Perfect as an 'extra' for a dinner party, this is another dish which originates from Hyderabad in southern India.

SERVES 4
10 ml (2 teaspoons) ground coriander
10 ml (2 teaspoons) ground cumin
10 ml (2 teaspoons) desiccated coconut
10 ml (2 tablespoons) sesame seeds
5 ml (1 teaspoon) mixed mustard and onion seeds
3 medium onions
300 ml ($\frac{1}{2}$ pint) oil
5 ml (1 teaspoon) fresh ginger, pulped
5 ml (1 teaspoon) fresh garlic, pulped
2.5 ml ($\frac{1}{2}$ teaspoon) turmeric
7.5 ml (1$\frac{1}{2}$ teaspoons) chilli powder
7.5 ml (1$\frac{1}{2}$ teaspoons) salt
3 medium aubergines, each slit four times
15 ml (1 tablespoon) tamarind paste
300 ml ($\frac{1}{2}$ pint) water
BAGHAAR
   150 ml ($\frac{1}{4}$ pint) oil
   5 ml (1 teaspoon) mixed onion and mustard seeds
   5 ml (1 teaspoon) cumin seeds
   4 dried red chillis
coriander leaves
green chilli
3 hard-boiled eggs

Roast the coriander, cumin, desiccated coconut, sesame seeds and mixed mustard and onion seeds together. Grind these in a food processor and leave aside. Peel and slice the onions.

In a large frying-pan heat the oil and fry the onions until golden brown. Lower the heat and add the ginger, garlic, turmeric, chilli powder and salt. Remove from the heat and allow to cool. Put this mixture into the food processor and chop to a paste. Remove from the processor. Blend the roast spices into the onion mixture, stuff the slit aubergines with this and leave aside.

In a separate bowl combine the tamarind paste and 45 ml (3 tablespoons) water to make a fine paste and leave aside.

In a separate saucepan heat the oil and fry the mixed onion and mustard seeds, cumin seeds and four dried red chillis. Lower the heat.

Gently drop the stuffed aubergines into the heated *baghaar* (oil dressing) and stir gently. Add the tamarind paste. Pour the water in and leave over a medium heat for 15–20 minutes. Add the fresh coriander leaves and green chillis.

When cool, transfer to a serving dish and serve decorated with three halved hard-boiled eggs.

Baingun bhurta
AUBERGINES & YOGHURT

This is an unusual dish, in that the aubergine is first baked in the oven, then cooked in a saucepan (using the *bhoono*-ing method).

SERVES 4
2 medium aubergines
60 ml (4 tablespoons) oil
1 medium onion
5 ml (1 teaspoon) white cumin seeds
5 ml (1 teaspoon) chilli powder
5 ml (1 teaspoon) salt
45 ml (3 tablespoons) natural yoghurt
2.5 ml (½ teaspoon) mint sauce
mint leaves to garnish

Wash and dry the aubergines and place in an ovenproof dish. Bake in a pre-heated oven, 160°C, 425°F, Gas 3, for 45 minutes. Remove from the oven and leave to cool. Peel and mash the aubergine.

In a saucepan heat the oil and fry the onions with the cumin seeds. Add all the spices, yoghurt and the mint sauce and stir together well. Put the aubergines over the onion mixture and stir-fry (using the *bhoono*-ing method) for 5–7 minutes or until the mixture is dry. Garnish with fresh mint.

Aloo matar
POTATOES & PEAS

This quick and easy-to-prepare vegetarian dish can be served either as an accompaniment or on its own with a *chapati*.

SERVES 2–4
3 medium onions
150 ml (¼ pint) oil
5 ml (1 teaspoon) fresh garlic, pulped
5 ml (1 teaspoon) fresh ginger, pulped
5 ml (1 teaspoon) chilli powder
2.5 ml (½ teaspoon) turmeric
5 ml (1 teaspoon) salt
2 green chillis
300 ml (½ pint) water
3 medium potatoes
100 g (4 oz) peas
fresh coriander leaves

Peel and slice the onions. Heat the oil and fry the onions until golden brown. Add all the spices and the green chillis, stir in 150 ml (¼ pint) water, cover and cook until the onions are cooked. Meanwhile, wash, peel and cut the potatoes into sixes. Add the potatoes and stir-fry for 5 minutes. Add the peas and the remaining 150 ml (¼ pint) water, cover and cook for 7–10 minutes. Serve garnished with fresh coriander leaves.

Dosa
RICE PANCAKES

Dosas (pancakes) are widely eaten in southern India. They can be served at almost any time of the day, either on their own with a chutney or served with a vegetable filling, when they are known as *masala dosa*.

MAKES 6–8
200 g (8 oz) rice and 50 g (2 oz) urid dhaal
or
200 g (8 oz) ground rice and 50 g (2 oz) urid dhaal flour (ata)
450–600 ml (¾–1 pint) water
5 ml (1 teaspoon) salt
60 ml (4 tablespoons) oil

Wash and pick over the rice and *dhaal* and soak for 3 hours. Grind the rice and urid dhaal to a smooth consistency, adding water if necessary. Leave aside for a further 3 hours to ferment. Alternatively, if you are using ground rice and urid dhaal flour (*ata*), mix together.

Add the water and salt and stir until batter-like in consistency. Heat about 15 ml (1 tablespoon) oil in a large, preferably non-stick, frying-pan. Using a deep spoon, pour the rice mixture into the frying-pan. Tilt the frying-pan to spread the mixture over the base. Cover and allow to cook for about 2 minutes over a medium heat. Remove the lid and turn the *dosa* over very carefully. Pour a little oil around the edge, cover and cook for a further 2 minutes. Serve warm with a chutney or, as *masala dosa*, with a filling (see below).

Masala dosa
STUFFED RICE PANCAKES

This recipe is simply the filling for the rice pancake (*dosa*) described in the last recipe.

4 medium potatoes
3 green chillis, chopped
2.5 ml ($\frac{1}{2}$ teaspoon) turmeric
5 ml (1 teaspoon) salt
150 ml ($\frac{1}{4}$ pint) oil
5 ml (1 teaspoon) mustard and onion seeds
3 dried red chillis
4 curry leaves
30 ml (2 tablespoons) lemon juice

Wash, peel and dice the potatoes. Boil the potatoes with the chopped green chillis, turmeric and salt until soft enough to be lightly mashed. Heat the oil in a saucepan and fry the mustard and onion seeds, dried red chillis and curry leaves for about 1 minute. Pour this *baghaar* over the potatoes, then sprinkle over the lemon juice. Spoon the potatoes over one half of the *dosa* and fold the other half over the potatoes. Serve hot with a chutney.
Note If desired, add a little cauliflower to the potatoes.

Thurai aur methi
COURGETTES & FRESH FENUGREEK LEAVES

This is one of the few curries for which I do not use fresh coriander, for the fresh fenugreek has a beautiful aroma and taste.

SERVES 4
90 ml (6 tablespoons) oil
1 medium onion
3 green chillis
5 ml (1 teaspoon) fresh ginger, pulped
5 ml (1 teaspoon) fresh garlic, pulped
5 ml (1 teaspoon) chilli powder
500 g (1 lb) courgettes
2 tomatoes
1 small bunch fenugreek

Heat the oil in a saucepan and fry the onion along with the green chillis and ginger, garlic and chilli powder. Add the sliced courgettes and the sliced tomatoes and stir-fry for 5–7 minutes. Add the washed fenugreek leaves and stir-fry for a further 5 minutes. Remove from the heat and serve hot with *chapati*.

Mili huwi subzee
MIXED VEGETABLES

This is one of my favourite vegetarian recipes. You can make it with any vegetables you choose, but I think the combination below is ideal.

SERVES 4
450 g (1 lb) onions
300 ml (½ pint) oil
5 ml (1 teaspoon) mustard seeds
5 ml (1 teaspoon) onion seeds
2.5 ml (½ teaspoon) white cumin seeds
3–4 curry leaves, chopped
3 medium tomatoes, chopped small
½ red, ½ green pepper, cut into small pieces
5 ml (1 teaspoon) fresh ginger pulp
5 ml (1 teaspoon) fresh garlic pulp
5 ml (1 teaspoon) chilli powder
1 ml (¼ teaspoon) turmeric
5 ml (1 teaspoon) salt
2 medium potatoes, peeled and cut into pieces
½ cauliflower, cut into small florets
4 medium carrots, peeled and sliced
450 ml (¾ pint) water
15 ml (1 tablespoon) lemon juice
3 green chillis, chopped
fresh coriander leaves

Peel and finely chop the onions and set aside. Heat the oil in a saucepan and fry the mustard, onion and white cumin seeds along with the curry leaves, until they turn a shade darker. Add the chopped onions and fry over a medium heat until golden brown. Add the tomatoes and the mixed red and green peppers. Stir-fry for about 5 minutes. Blend in all the spices and mix well. Add 300 ml (½ pint) water, cover and simmer for 10–12 minutes, stirring occasionally. Add all the remaining vegetables, green chillis and fresh coriander and stir-fry for about 5 minutes. Add the remaining 150 ml (¼ pint) water and the lemon juice. Cover and simmer for about 15 minutes, stirring occasionally.

CHAPTER 7
Chicken (murgh)

In India chicken is expensive and is therefore considered a special-occasion meat. A chicken dish is invariably served at every special function. Indians almost always cook chicken skinned and cut into small pieces. If the chicken weighs about 1.5 kg (3 lb) it should be cut into about 8 pieces, unless you are making tandoori chicken, when chicken quarters look a lot better and are more appropriate. This is where I have always found the Indian and Pakistani butchers extremely helpful, as they will skin, cut and even bone the chicken if required.

Murgh kali mirch
CHICKEN TOSSED IN BLACK PEPPER

Using black pepper instead of chilli powder produces a milder curry. This recipe is basically a stir-fry one and can be prepared in a short time. The dish goes well with fried corn and peas (page 120).

SERVES 4–6
1.5 kg (3 lb) chicken, cut into 8
5 ml (1 teaspoon) fresh ginger, pulped
5 ml (1 teaspoon) fresh garlic, pulped
5 ml (1 teaspoon) salt
7.5 ml (1½ teaspoons) coarsely ground black pepper
150 ml (¼ pint) oil
1 green pepper, roughly sliced
150 ml (¼ pint) water
30 ml (2 tablespoons) lemon juice

Bone the chicken for this dish if you prefer. Combine the ginger, garlic, salt and coarsely ground black pepper together with the chicken and leave aside. Heat the oil in a large saucepan and add the chicken. Stir-fry for 10 minutes. Lower the heat, add the green pepper and the water. Simmer for 10 minutes and sprinkle over the lemon juice.

Kadahi murgh
BONED CHICKEN DEEP-FRIED WITH HERBS & SPICES

One of my favourite dinner-party dishes, this is very attractive to look at. It should ideally be cooked and served from a *karahi*, but if you do not have one a deep, heavy frying-pan will do. As this is a dry dish I always serve a wet curry with it, together with a *raita* (yoghurt sauce).

SERVES 4
1.5 kg (3 lb) chicken, boned and cut into 8
7.5 ml (1½ teaspoons) fresh garlic, pulped
7.5 ml (1½ teaspoons) fresh ginger, pulped
5 ml (1 teaspoon) salt
2 medium onions
½ large bunch fresh coriander leaves
4–6 green chillis
600 ml (1 pint) oil
4 firm tomatoes
2 large green peppers

Wash the chicken pieces, rub the ginger, garlic and salt over the chicken pieces and leave aside. Peel and chop the onions, grind half the onions with the coriander leaves and the green chillis and rub this over the chicken pieces. Heat the oil in a *karahi* or large frying-pan and fry the other half of the onions until golden brown. Remove the onions from the pan with a slotted spoon and leave aside. Lower the heat to medium and fry the chicken pieces about two at a time until cooked through (about 5–7 minutes per piece).

Meanwhile cut the tomatoes into wedges and roughly cut the green peppers. When all the chicken pieces are cooked return them to the pan, add the tomatoes and the peppers and half-cook them. Garnish with fried onions and serve direct from the pan.

Murgh makhani
BUTTERED CHICKEN

A simple and mouth-watering dish with a lovely thick sauce, this makes an impressive centrepiece for a dinner party.

SERVES 4–6
10 ml (2 teaspoons) garam masala
10 ml (2 teaspoons) ground coriander
5 ml (1 teaspoon) fresh ginger, pulped
5 ml (1 teaspoon) chilli powder
5 ml (1 teaspoon) black cumin seeds
5 ml (1 teaspoon) fresh garlic, pulped
5 ml (1 teaspoon) salt
3 whole green cardamoms
3 whole black peppercorns
2 medium onions
100 g (4 oz) unsalted butter
15 ml (1 tablespoon) oil
150 ml (5 fl oz) natural yoghurt
30 ml (2 tablespoons) tomato purée
1.5 kg (3 lb) chicken, skinned and cut into 8
150 ml ($\frac{1}{4}$ pint) water
2 whole bay leaves
150 ml (5 oz) single cream
GARNISH
   coriander leaves
   2 green chillis

Prepare all the spices. Finely chop the onions. Heat the butter with 15 ml (1 tablespoon) oil. Fry the onions until golden brown. Lower the heat.

In a separate bowl blend together all the spices (except the bay leaves), the yoghurt, tomato purée and chicken pieces. Add this to the onions and *bhoono* (stir vigorously making semi-circular movements) for 5–7 minutes. Add the water and the bay leaves and simmer for 30 minutes stirring occasionally. Add the cream and cook for a further 10–15 minutes.

Garnish with fresh coriander leaves and chopped green chillis.

Murgh dopiaza
CHICKEN & ONIONS

This dish represents one of the rare occasions when we do not use yoghurt to cook chicken. It has a lovely flavour and is perfect served with *pulao* rice. It also freezes very well.

SERVES 4
300 ml (½ pint) oil
4 medium onions, finely chopped
7.5 ml (1½ teaspoons) fresh ginger, pulped
7.5 ml (1½ teaspoons) garam masala
7.5 ml (1½ teaspoons) fresh garlic, pulped
5 ml (1 teaspoon) chilli powder
5 ml (1 teaspoon) ground coriander
3 whole cardamoms
3 peppercorns
45 ml (3 tablespoons) tomato purée
1.5 kg (3 lb) chicken, cut into 8
300 ml (½ pint) water
30 ml (2 tablespoons) lemon juice
green chilli
fresh coriander leaves

Heat the oil in a large saucepan and fry the finely chopped onion until golden brown. Lower the heat and add all the spices and the tomato purée. Stir-fry for 5–7 minutes. Add the chicken pieces and blend together. Put the water into the saucepan, cover and simmer for 20–25 minutes. Add the lemon juice sparingly and the green chilli and finely chopped coriander. Serve hot.

Murgh khorma
CHICKEN KHORMA

Chicken *khorma* is one of the most popular curries, especially in Britain, and this one is perfect for a dinner party.

SERVES 4–6
7.5 ml (1½ teaspoons) fresh ginger, pulped
7.5 ml (1½ teaspoons) fresh garlic, pulped
10 ml (2 teaspoons) garam masala
5 ml (1 teaspoon) chilli powder
5 ml (1 teaspoon) salt
5 ml (1 teaspoon) black cumin seeds
3 green cardamoms, with husks removed and seeds crushed
5 ml (1 teaspoon) ground coriander
5 ml (1 teaspoon) ground almonds
150 ml (5 fl oz) natural yoghurt
1.5 kg (3 lb) chicken, skinned and cut into 8
300 ml (½ pint) oil
2 medium onions, sliced
150 ml (¼ pint) water
fresh coriander
green chillis, chopped

Prepare all the spices, mix with the yoghurt, rub over the chicken pieces and leave aside. Heat the oil in a large saucepan and fry the sliced onions until golden brown. Gradually add the chicken pieces, stir-frying continuously (using the *bhoono*-ing method) for 5–7 minutes. Add the water, cover and simmer on a low heat for 20–25 minutes. Add the fresh coriander leaves and chopped green chillis and cook for a further 10 minutes, stirring gently from time to time.

Tandoori murgh
TANDOORI-STYLE CHICKEN

Undoubtedly the most popular of all chicken dishes, tandoori chicken is delicious
barbecued in the summer months. As we cannot all have *tandoor* (clay) ovens, what I do is
pre-heat the grill to a very high temperature then lower it to medium to cook this dish.
Serve the succulent chicken pieces garnished with a few onion rings and sliced tomatoes on
a bed of lettuce with lemon wedges. *Naan* and mint *raita* complement the dish perfectly.

SERVES 4
4 chicken quarters, skinned
150 ml (5 fl oz) natural yoghurt
7.5 ml (1½ teaspoons) fresh ginger, pulped
7.5 ml (1½ teaspoons) fresh garlic, pulped
5 ml (1 teaspoon) chilli powder
10 ml (2 teaspoons) ground cumin
10 ml (2 teaspoons) ground coriander
5 ml (1 teaspoon) salt
2.5 ml (½ teaspoon) red colouring
15 ml (1 tablespoon) tamarind paste
150 ml (¼ pint) water
150 ml (¼ pint) oil

Marinate the chicken in the yoghurt, with all the spices and colouring, well blended in a large
bowl, for a minimum of 3 hours.

In a separate bowl mix the tamarind paste with the water with a fork and fold this into the
yoghurt. Rub this over the chicken pieces and leave aside for 3 hours. Place the chicken pieces
in a heatproof dish. Brush the top with oil. Pre-heat the grill, turn the heat to medium and place
the chicken under the grill, not too close to the heat. Grill for 30–35 minutes, turning twice and
basting with the remaining oil.

Arrange on a bed of lettuce and garnish with onion rings, sliced tomatoes and lemon
wedges.

Dum ki murgh
SPICY ROAST CHICKEN

This chicken dish, ideal for dinner parties, is cooked in the oven – which is very rare in Indian cooking. The chicken can be boned if desired.

SERVES 4

50g (2oz) ground almonds
50g (2oz) desiccated coconut
150ml ($\frac{1}{4}$ pint) oil
1 medium onion, finely chopped
5ml (1 teaspoon) fresh ginger, pulped
5ml (1 teaspoon) fresh garlic, pulped
5ml (1 teaspoon) chilli powder
7.5ml (1$\frac{1}{2}$ teaspoons) garam masala
5ml (1 teaspoon) salt
150ml (5fl oz) yoghurt
4 chicken quarters, skinned
coriander leaves
1 lemon, cut into wedges

In a heavy saucepan roast the ground almonds and coconut and leave aside. Heat the oil and fry the finely chopped onion until golden brown. Remove from the heat. Blend all the spices into the yoghurt, including the ground almonds and coconut. Combine this with the onion and leave aside. In an ovenproof dish arrange the washed and skinned chicken quarters and pour the spice mixture over the chicken sparingly. Place the dish in a pre-heated oven 160°C, 425°F, Gas 3 for 35–45 minutes. Before serving, pierce with a skewer or a sharp knife to check that the chicken is cooked right through. Sprinkle the coriander leaves over and serve with lemon wedges.

Murgh tikka
CHICKEN TIKKA

For this very popular dish, small pieces of boned chicken are marinated either overnight or for a minimum of 3 hours in yoghurt and spices. Chicken tikka can either be served with *naan, raita* and mango chutney or as a starter.

SERVES 6
5 ml (1 teaspoon) fresh ginger, pulped
5 ml (1 teaspoon) fresh garlic, pulped
7.5 ml (1½ teaspoons) ground coriander
7.5 ml (1½ teaspoons) ground cumin
5 ml (1 teaspoon) chilli powder
45 ml (3 tablespoons) yoghurt
5 ml (1 teaspoon) salt
30 ml (2 tablespoons) lemon juice
a few drops red colouring (optional)
15 ml (1 tablespoon) tomato purée
1.5 kg (3 lb) chicken, boned and cut into 8
1 onion, sliced
45 ml (3 tablespoons) oil
GARNISH
   1 lemon, cut into wedges
   6 lettuce leaves

In a large mixing bowl blend all the spices together with the yoghurt, salt, lemon juice, colouring and tomato purée. Add the chicken pieces to the spice mixture and coat well. Leave overnight, or for at least 3 hours.

In a heatproof dish arrange the sliced onion and pour half the oil on to this. Lay the chicken pieces on top of the onions and grill under a pre-heated grill on a medium heat for 25–30 minutes. Baste with the remaining oil, turning the pieces once. Serve on a bed of lettuce and garnish with the lemon wedges.

CHAPTER 8
Kebabs

Many non-Indians think all kebabs are served on skewers, but in fact only one of the recipes that follow is for skewered kebabs (*sheekh* kebabs). A kebab is basically a type of rissole, made of minced or cubed meat and shaped into a round or, in the case of *shaami* kebabs, an oval with pointed ends.

If you are serving kebabs, which are dry, you will probably wish to offer a wetter dish – perhaps a *dhaal*, a vegetable curry or a meat curry with a good sauce – as part of the same meal.

Sheekh kebabs
KEBABS COOKED ON SKEWERS

These minced lamb kebabs should ideally be barbecued, on skewers, but I use my grill – especially in the winter. They can be served as a starter or as part of a full-scale meal.

MAKES 10–12
meat tenderizer
500 g (1 lb) lean minced lamb
1 medium onion
2 green chillis
coriander leaves
5 ml (1 teaspoon) fresh ginger, pulped
5 ml (1 teaspoon) fresh garlic, pulped
5 ml (1 teaspoon) ground cumin
5 ml (1 teaspoon) ground coriander
2.5 ml (½ teaspoon) salt
5 ml (1 teaspoon) chilli powder
2.5 ml (1 teaspoon) ground allspice
5 ml (1 teaspoon) garam masala
30 ml (2 tablespoons) yoghurt

Apply the meat tenderizer to the lean minced lamb with your fingers and blend in well. Leave aside for at least 3 hours. Meanwhile peel and finely chop the onion, green chillis and coriander leaves and mix well together. Add the ginger, garlic, ground cumin, ground coriander, salt, chilli powder, ground allspice and garam masala to the yoghurt. Blend all this with the onion mixture.

Blend into the mince and mix together with your hand. Divide into 10–12 equal portions. Roll round the skewers with your fingers, gently pressing all round. Grill under a pre-heated grill on the middle shelf over a medium heat, basting with the oil occasionally. Serve garnished with onion rings and lemon wedges accompanied by a *raita*.

Shaami kebabs
MEAT KEBABS

All my friends like this dish, which, like kebabs of any sort, is always handy to have in the freezer. It is best served with the rice dish *bagara khana* (page 101) and a *dhaal* or a wet vegetable curry. This particular kebab also makes very good sandwich spread, either in *paratas* or between a couple of slices of bread.

MAKES 10–12
45 ml (3 tablespoons) chana dhaal
450 g (1 lb) lean lamb, boned and cubed
5 ml (1 teaspoon) fresh ginger, pulped
5 ml (1 teaspoon) fresh garlic, pulped
5 ml (1 teaspoon) chilli powder
7.5 ml (1½ teaspoons) salt
7.5 ml (1½ teaspoons) garam masala
3 green chillis
fresh coriander leaves
1 medium onion, peeled and chopped
300 ml (½ pint) oil
900 ml (1½ pints) water
30 ml (2 tablespoons) natural yoghurt
1 medium egg
GARNISH
   onion rings and green chillis

Wash the chana dhaal twice carefully, removing any stones or other impurities. Boil the chana dhaal until the water dries up completely and it is soft enough to be mashed to a paste in a food processor. Mix all the meat and spices in a bowl along with two green chillis, half of the fresh coriander leaves and the peeled and chopped onion. In a saucepan heat 30 ml (2 tablespoons) of the oil, put the meat mixture into the saucepan and add 900 ml (1½ pints) water and cook, covered, over a low heat for 45–60 minutes. Check to see whether the meat is tender enough to be mashed to a paste in the food processor. Evaporate any excess water by taking the lid off and cooking for a further 10–15 minutes. Once the meat has been mashed, blend the yoghurt, one egg, the mashed chana dhaal paste, finely chopped green chilli and the fresh coriander leaves. Mix together with your fingers. Break off small balls of the meat paste and make small, flat circular shapes – about 12 – with the palms of your hands. Heat the oil in a frying-pan and gently drop in the *shaami* kebabs, about three at a time, and fry, turning once. Serve garnished with onion rings and green chillis.
Note Substitute beef for lamb in this dish if preferred.

Murgh kebabs
CHICKEN KEBABS

These kebabs are a deliciously different way of serving chicken, and they freeze well. Serve with any *dhaal* and *chapati*.

SERVES 6–8
1.5 kg (3 lb) boned chicken
7.5 ml (1½ teaspoons) ground cumin
4 cardamom seeds, crushed
2.5 ml (½ teaspoon) ground cinnamon
5 ml (1 teaspoon) salt
5 ml (1 teaspoon) fresh ginger, pulped
5 ml (1 teaspoon) fresh garlic, pulped
2.5 ml (½ teaspoon) ground allspice
2.5 ml (½ teaspoon) ground black pepper
300 ml (½ pint) water
30 ml (2 tablespoons) yoghurt
2 green chillis
1 small onion
fresh coriander leaves
1 medium egg, beaten
300 ml (½ pint) oil

Boil the boned chicken with all the spices in 300 ml (½ pint) water until the water has been absorbed. Put this mixture in a food processor and grind to a paste. Remove from the processor and place in a bowl. Add the yoghurt and blend together. Place the green chillis, onion and coriander leaves in the food processor and grind finely. Add to the chicken mixture. Add the beaten egg. Break off 12–15 equal portions and make small, flat round shapes in the palm of your hand. When all are ready heat the oil in a saucepan and fry the kebabs gently over a low heat, turning once. Drain on kitchen paper.

Kheemay kay kebab
MINCED LAMB KEBABS

There are many ways of cooking kebabs. In this particular recipe you cook the mince before making the kebabs. This sort can be served with any curry or a *dhaal*. They also freeze very well and can be re-heated under the grill or in the oven.

SERVES 6–8
15 ml (1 tablespoon) chana dhaal
500 g (1 lb) lean minced lamb
1 medium onion, sliced
5 ml (1 teaspoon) fresh ginger, pulped
5 ml (1 teaspoon) fresh garlic, pulped
5 ml (1 teaspoon) chilli powder
5 ml (1 teaspoon) salt
2 black peppercorns
5 ml (1 teaspoon) white cumin seeds
5 ml (1 teaspoon) coriander seeds
2 dried red chillis
120 ml (4 fl oz) water
coriander leaves
1 large egg
170 ml (6 fl oz) oil

Soak the chana dhaal in warm water for about 3 hours. Make into a paste and leave aside. Place the minced lamb, sliced onion and all the other spices in a medium-sized saucepan. Stir and mix with a spoon. Add the water and cook over a medium heat for 15–20 minutes, stirring occasionally. When the water has evaporated, turn off the heat and leave to cool. When the mixture has cooled, place it in a food processor along with the chana dhaal paste and grind the mince to form a paste-like consistency. Return the mixture to the pan and add the finely chopped coriander leaves. Break off small balls of the mixture and make small flat round shapes, using the palms of your hand. Beat the egg in a separate bowl. Heat the oil in a frying-pan, dip the kebabs into the egg and fry over a medium heat until golden brown.

Boti kebabs
CUBED LAMB KEBABS

These kebabs are very popular in India and Pakistan. I simply love these and remember going out in the evenings just to have *boti* kebabs sitting out in the open. (*Boti* kebabs are barbecued as you watch, to order).

SERVES 6–8
1 kg (2 lb) lean lamb, boned and cubed
5 ml (1 teaspoon) meat tenderizer
7.5 ml (1½ teaspoons) fresh ginger, pulped
7.5 ml (1½ teaspoons) fresh garlic, pulped
5 ml (1 teaspoon) chilli powder
2.5 ml (½ teaspoon) turmeric
2.5 ml (½ teaspoon) salt
30 ml (2 tablespoons) water
8 tomatoes, cut in half
8 small pickling onions
10 mushrooms
1 green pepper, cut into large pieces
1 red pepper, cut into large pieces
30 ml (2 tablespoons) cooking oil
2 lemons, cut into quarters

Wash the meat and place in a clean dish. Apply the tenderizer to the meat, using your hands. Leave for about 3 hours at room temperature. Mix all the spices in a cup with about 30 ml (2 tablespoons) water and rub over the meat until it is coated with the spices. Arrange the meat on skewers with the vegetables and peppers and brush with oil. Grill under a pre-heated grill for 25–30 minutes or until the meat is cooked right through. When cooked, remove from the grill and place the skewers on a plate. Arrange lemon wedges on the side and serve immediately with rice and a *raita*.

Chaplee kebabs
MINCED LAMB KEBABS WITH POMEGRANATE SEEDS

The pomegranate seeds used in this Peshwari recipe give these kebabs a tangy flavour that makes them different from other kinds. You can serve them in a bun (like a beefburger) for a free-and-easy Saturday lunch.

SERVES 6; MAKES 10–12
450g (1 lb) minced lamb
6 medium spring onions
2 small tomatoes
fresh coriander leaves
1–2 green chillis
2.5 ml ($\frac{1}{2}$ teaspoon) dried red chillis
4 black peppercorns
2.5 ml ($\frac{1}{2}$ teaspoon) coriander seeds
5 ml (1 teaspoon) fresh ginger, pulped
5 ml (1 teaspoon) fresh garlic, pulped
5 ml (1 teaspoon) salt
5 ml (1 teaspoon) pomegranate seeds
15 ml (1 tablespoon) plain flour
15 ml (1 tablespoon) gram flour

Place the minced lamb in a large mixing bowl. Finely chop the onions, tomatoes, fresh coriander leaves and green chillis. Crush the red chillis and peppercorns and coarsely grind the coriander seeds. Add all the spices and other ingredients to the minced lamb and mix well, using your hand. If the mixture is not fine enough, put the mixture in the food processor and chop once. Break off small balls, the size of a golf ball, and make flat, round shapes in the palm of your hand. Leave aside. In a heavy frying-pan heat the oil and gently drop in the kebabs. Lower the heat and fry these, pressing with a flat spoon and turning twice. Drain the kebabs on kitchen paper.

Dum ka kheema
GRILLED MINCED LAMB

This is rather an unusual way of cooking mince. In India this is cooked on a naked flame, but I use my grill instead and find it works just as well.

SERVES 4
75 ml (5 tablespoons) oil
2 medium onions, sliced
450 g (1 lb) minced lamb
30 ml (2 tablespoons) yoghurt
5 ml (1 teaspoon) chilli powder
5 ml (1 teaspoon) fresh ginger, pulped
5 ml (1 teaspoon) fresh garlic, pulped
5 ml (1 teaspoon) salt
7.5 ml (1½ teaspoons) garam masala
2.5 ml (¼ teaspoon) ground allspice
2 fresh green chillis
fresh coriander
GARNISH
   1 onion, cut into rings
   coriander leaves
   1 lemon, cut into wedges

Heat the oil in a saucepan and fry the onions until golden brown. In a large bowl mix the minced lamb with the yoghurt and all the other spices and add to the fried onion. Stir-fry for 10–15 minutes. Turn the heat off and leave to cool. Meanwhile, put the green chillis and half of the coriander leaves into a food processor and grind. Remove and leave aside. Put the mince through the food processor and grind. Remove, mix with the green chillis and coriander leaves and blend together. Transfer this on to a heatproof shallow dish. Pre-heat the grill, then grill under a medium heat for 10–15 minutes, moving it about with a fork. Watch it carefully to prevent burning. Serve garnished with onion rings, chopped coriander leaves and lemon wedges.

Potato cutlets

The minced lamb used in these cutlets is seasoned with black pepper instead of chilli powder, which gives them a different flavour. They can either be served with a *dhaal* and *chapati* or with the hot salad described on page 118.

SERVES 4–6
5 medium potatoes
10 ml (2 teaspoons) salt
360 ml (13 fl oz) oil
1 medium onion, sliced
5 ml (1 teaspoon) fresh ginger, pulped
5 ml (1 teaspoon) fresh garlic, pulped
5 ml (1 teaspoon) coarsely ground black pepper
500 g (1 lb) minced lamb
coriander leaves
100 g (4 oz) breadcrumbs

Peel, boil and mash the potatoes. Add 5 ml (1 teaspoon) salt and leave aside to cool. Heat 60 ml (4 tablespoons) oil and fry the sliced onion until golden brown. Add all the spices and the minced lamb and stir-fry for 10–15 minutes. Add the fresh coriander leaves and leave aside. Divide the mashed potato into 10 equal portions and flatten each in the palm of your hand. Put about 15 ml (1 tablespoon) of the minced lamb in the centre and fold the potato over this. Gently pat into a round shape and leave aside. Dip the cutlets lightly into the breadcrumbs. Heat 300 ml ($\frac{1}{2}$ pint) oil in a heavy saucepan and shallow-fry the cutlets until golden brown, turning once. Drain on kitchen paper.

CHAPTER 9

Lentils (dhaals)

There are at least thirty different types of lentil to be found in India, but the four most commonly used are moong, masoor, chana and urid, each of which is described in the glossary. Some of the lentils are whole, while others are split. Lentils are very versatile and can be cooked in many different ways. Rich in protein, they make ideal accompaniments to vegetable curries, which otherwise lack protein.

Lentils are also delicious cooked with meat and served with lemon wedges, garnished with fresh coriander leaves and shredded ginger.

Before cooking, wash the lentils at least twice and pick over carefully to remove any pieces of grit. It is not strictly necessary to soak them, but if you have time soak them for three hours to cut down on cooking time. Boil the lentils in twice the volume of water.

Khadi dhaal
ONION DHAAL

This *dhaal* is semi-dry when cooked so it is best to serve it with a curry which has a sauce. Ordinary onions can be used as a substitute if spring onions are not available.

SERVES 4
100 g (4 oz) masoor dhaal
90 ml (6 tablespoons) oil
1 small bunch spring onions, trimmed and
   chopped, including the green part
5 ml (1 teaspoon) fresh ginger, pulped
5 ml (1 teaspoon) fresh garlic, pulped
2.5 ml ($\frac{1}{2}$ teaspoon) chilli powder
2.5 ml ($\frac{1}{2}$ teaspoon) turmeric
300 ml ($\frac{1}{2}$ pint) water
5 ml (1 teaspoon) salt
1 green chilli, chopped
fresh coriander leaves

Wash the lentils and leave aside. In a saucepan heat the oil and fry the chopped spring onions. Lower the heat and add all the spices (not the salt). Stir-fry the onions with the spices. Blend in the lentils and add the water. Lower the heat further and cook for 20–25 minutes. When cooked add the salt and mix it in gently with a spoon.

Garnish with the chopped green chilli and fresh coriander leaves.

Chahni huwi dhaal aur kofteh
STRAINED DHAAL WITH MEATBALLS

This is a *dhaal* with a difference. After cooking it I put meatballs (*koftas*) in it and a few fried potato wafers. Serve it with fried rice (*bagara khana*, page 101) or plain boiled rice and poppadoms.

SERVES 6–8
200 g (8 oz) masoor dhaal
5 ml (1 teaspoon) fresh ginger, pulped
5 ml (1 teaspoon) fresh garlic, pulped
2.5 ml ($\frac{1}{2}$ teaspoon) turmeric
7.5 ml ($1\frac{1}{2}$ teaspoons) chilli powder
900 ml ($1\frac{1}{2}$ pints) water
7.5 ml ($1\frac{1}{2}$ teaspoons) salt
45 ml (3 tablespoons) lemon juice
3 green chillis
fresh coriander leaves
BAGHAAR
   150 ml ($\frac{1}{4}$ pint) oil
   3 garlic cloves
   4 dried red chillis
   5 ml (1 teaspoon) white cumin seeds
POTATO FRIES
   2 medium potatoes
   1 pinch salt
   300 ml ($\frac{1}{2}$ pint) oil

Wash and pick over the *dhaal* and boil with the ginger, garlic, turmeric and chilli powder until soft and mushy. Add the salt. Mash the *dhaal*, preferably with a wooden masher, and put through a sieve. Add the lemon juice to the strained liquid. Chop the green chillis and fresh coriander leaves and set aside. Stir 300 ml ($\frac{1}{2}$ pint) water into the strained liquid and bring to the boil over a low heat. Remove from the heat and leave aside. Meanwhile make the *koftas* and drop them gently into the *dhaal*. (For the meat *koftas*, follow the recipe for *shaami* kebabs, page 81, but shape into small balls rather than flat rounds.)

Prepare the *baghaar* by heating the oil and frying the ingredients for 2 minutes. Remove from the heat and pour over the *dhaal*.

For the potato fries, wash, peel and slice the potatoes thinly. Rub the salt over them. Heat the oil in a frying-pan and fry the potatoes until crisp.

Decorate the *dhaal* with the fried potatoes and garnish with the green chillis and fresh coriander leaves.

Lobia
BLACK-EYE BEANS

This is semi-dry when cooked, and is very good served with a few drops of lemon juice or with *chapati* and a wet curry.

SERVES 4
150g (6oz) lobia (black-eye beans)
2 medium onions
300ml ($\frac{1}{2}$ pint) oil
5ml (1 teaspoon) fresh ginger, pulped
5ml (1 teaspoon) fresh garlic, pulped
5ml (1 teaspoon) chilli powder
7.5ml (1$\frac{1}{2}$ teaspoons) salt
7.5ml (1$\frac{1}{2}$ teaspoons) ground coriander
7.5ml (1$\frac{1}{2}$ teaspoons) ground cumin
150ml ($\frac{1}{4}$ pint) water
2 green chillis
fresh coriander leaves
15ml (1 tablespoon) lemon juice

Wash and soak the black-eye beans in plenty of water overnight. Boil over a low heat for about 30 minutes, drain and leave aside. Peel and slice the onions, heat the oil and fry them until golden brown. Add all the spices and stir-fry for 3–5 minutes. Add the water, cover and cook until the water has evaporated. Add the boiled black-eye beans, the green chillis and the coriander leaves and blend together. Stir-fry for 3–5 minutes. Remove from the heat and transfer to a serving dish. Sprinkle over the lemon juice and serve hot or cold.

Maash ki dhaal
WHITE LENTILS

This *dhaal* is dry when cooked, so I always give it a *baghaar*, or seasoned oil dressing. It makes an excellent accompaniment to any meal of *khorma* and *chapati*.

SERVES 2–4
100g (4oz) urid dhaal
600ml (1 pint) water
5ml (1 teaspoon) fresh ginger, pulped
5ml (1 teaspoon salt
5ml (1 teaspoon) coarsely ground black pepper
30ml (2 tablespoons) pure or vegetable ghee
2 cloves garlic, peeled
2 green chillis, chopped
mint leaves for garnish

Wash the lentils twice, removing any stones.

In a separate saucepan heat the ghee and add the cloves of garlic and chopped green chillis. Pour this *baghaar* over the *dhaal* and garnish with the mint leaves. Serve hot with *chapati*.

Tarka dhaal
OIL-DRESSED DHAAL

This *dhaal* is given a *tarka*, or *baghaar* (seasoned oil dressing), just before serving, of ghee, onion and a combination of seeds. It has a thick sauce when cooked. It makes a very good accompaniment, especially for a dry vegetarian or meat curry, and will freeze well (just re-heat in a saucepan or covered in the oven).

SERVES 4
75g (3oz) masoor dhaal
50g (2oz) moong dhaal
450ml (¾ pint) water
5ml (1 teaspoon) fresh ginger, pulped
5ml (1 teaspoon) fresh garlic, pulped
2 green chillis, chopped
5ml (1 teaspoon) salt
TARKA (BAGHAAR)
   30ml (2 tablespoons) ghee
   1 medium onion, sliced
   mixed mustard and onion seeds
GARNISH
   fresh coriander leaves, finely chopped

Wash and pick over the *dhaals* to remove any stones. Boil the *dhaals* together over a medium heat with the ginger, garlic and green chillis, half covered with a lid, until they are cooked enough to be mashed (about 15–20 minutes). Mash the *dhaals* and add more water if necessary to form a thick sauce. Add the salt and leave aside. Transfer to a heatproof serving dish. Just before serving, melt the ghee in a small saucepan, add the sliced onion and fry until golden brown. Add the mixed seeds and just pour this while hot over the *dhaal*.

Garnish with the coriander leaves and serve immediately.

Palak aur chanay ki dhaal
SPINACH & CHANA DHAAL

An attractive-looking dish, this makes a good vegetarian accompaniment to almost any meal, but for a good contrast in colour and taste I usually cook a tomato curry with this.

SERVES 4–6
60 ml (4 tablespoons) chana dhaal
90 ml (6 tablespoons) oil
5 ml (1 teaspoon) mixed onion and mustard seeds
4 dried red chillis
400–450 g (14–16 oz) canned spinach
5 ml (1 teaspoon) fresh ginger, pulped
5 ml (1 teaspoon) ground coriander
5 ml (1 teaspoon) ground cumin
5 ml (1 teaspoon) salt
5 ml (1 teaspoon) chilli powder
30 ml (2 tablespoons) lemon juice
1 green chilli

Soak the chana dhaal, ideally overnight or for at least 3 hours in warm water, then boil for $\frac{1}{2}$ hour. Heat the oil in a saucepan and fry the mixed seeds and dried red chillis. Add the drained spinach, all the spices and the salt and chilli powder and lower the heat. Stir-fry for 7–10 minutes. Add the chana dhaal and blend into the spinach well by stirring gently so that it does not break up. Turn the heat off. Transfer the mixture to a serving dish. Sprinkle over the lemon juice and garnish with the green chilli.

Sookhi moong dhaal
DRY MOONG DHAAL

I like to give this dhaal a *baghaar* (seasoned oil dressing) of butter, dried red chillis and white cumin seeds. It is simple to cook and tastes very good.

SERVES 4
150 g (6 oz) moong dhaal
5 ml (1 teaspoon) fresh ginger, pulped
2,5 ml ($\frac{1}{2}$ teaspoon) ground cumin
2.5 ml ($\frac{1}{2}$ teaspoon) ground coriander
5 ml (1 teaspoon) fresh garlic, pulped
2.5 ml ($\frac{1}{2}$ teaspoon) chilli powder
600 ml (1 pint) water
5 ml (1 teaspoon) salt

BAGHAAR

   100 g (4 oz) unsalted butter
   5 dried red chillis
   5 ml (1 teaspoon) white cumin seeds

Wash and pick over the *dhaal*, add all the spices and cook over a medium heat covered with the water until the lentils are soft but not mushy. Add the salt, stir and mix gently with a spoon. Set aside. Melt the butter and fry the dried red chillis and white cumin seeds until they begin to pop. Remove from the heat, pour the *baghaar* over the *dhaal* and serve immediately with *chapati* and any meat or vegetable curry.

Khatti dhaal
LEMON DHAAL

This *dhaal* is eaten almost every day in most households in Hyderabad in India. Traditionally it is cooked with tamarind but I like to use lemon juice instead, which is not only easier but gives it a better colour. It is a good accompaniment to *badaami khorma* (lamb *khorma* with almonds).

SERVES 4
100 g (4 oz) masoor dhaal
5 ml (1 teaspoon) fresh ginger, pulped
5 ml (1 teaspoon) fresh garlic, pulped
5 ml (1 teaspoon) chilli powder
2.5 ml ($\frac{1}{2}$ teaspoon) turmeric
450 ml ($\frac{3}{4}$ pint) water
5 ml (1 teaspoon) salt
45 ml (3 tablespoons) lemon juice
2 green chillis
coriander leaves
BAGHAAR
   150 ml ($\frac{1}{4}$ pint) oil
   4 whole garlic cloves
   6 dried red chillis
   5 ml (1 teaspoon) white cumin seeds

Wash and pick through the masoor dhaal carefully. Add the ginger, garlic, chilli powder and turmeric to the *dhaal*, stir in 300 ml ($\frac{1}{2}$ pint) water and boil over a medium heat with the lid left slightly open until the *dhaal* is soft enough to be mashed. Mash the *dhaal*, preferably with a wooden masher, and add the salt, lemon juice and 150 ml ($\frac{1}{4}$ pint) water, stir and mix well. It should be of the same consistency as cream of chicken soup, though not necessarily as smooth. Add the green chillis and fresh coriander leaves and set aside. In a separate frying-pan prepare the *baghaar* by heating the oil and adding all the *baghaar* ingredients. Fry for about 1 minute. Turn off the heat. When a little cooler pour the *baghaar* over the *dhaal*. If the *dhaal* is too runny just cook over a medium heat with the lid off for a further 3–5 minutes. Serve hot.

CHAPTER 10

Seafood and Fish

India may not be thought of as a great fish-eating nation, but there are certain parts of it, notably Bengal and around the city of Karachi, where fish is very popular. Indeed, the staple diet of the Bengalis is fish and rice; they enjoy river fish from the Hooghli and also lobster and king prawns, and they tend to use mustard oil a lot when cooking it. Prawns are eaten all over India and Pakistan even in areas far from the sea because you can buy them in a dried form, in packets.

Bengali machli

BENGALI-STYLE FISH

Fresh fish is eaten a great deal in Bengal (Bangladesh), and this dish is made with mustard oil which gives the fish a good flavour.

SERVES 4–6
5 ml (1 teaspoon) turmeric
5 ml (1 teaspoon) salt
1 kg (2 lb) cod fillet
90 ml (6 tablespoons) corn oil
4 green chillis
5 ml (1 teaspoon) fresh ginger, pulped
5 ml (1 teaspoon) fresh garlic, pulped
2 medium onions, finely chopped
2 tomatoes, finely chopped
90 ml (6 tablespoons) mustard oil
water
coriander leaves, chopped, for garnish

Rub the turmeric and salt on the fish pieces. Heat the oil in a frying-pan and fry the fish lightly until pale yellow. Remove and set aside.

Combine the green chillis and all remaining ingredients except the coriander leaves in a food processor and grind to a fine paste. Transfer the paste to a saucepan and fry until golden brown. Remove from the heat and gently drop the fish pieces into the paste without breaking. Return to the heat, add 450 ml (¾ pint) water and cook, uncovered, over a medium/low heat for 15–20 minutes. Serve garnished with fresh coriander leaves.

Besun may thali huwi machli
FRIED FISH IN GRAM FLOUR

Very simple to make, this fried fish dish goes very well with *tamatar ki chutney* and *bagara khana*.

SERVES 4–6
100g (4oz) gram flour
5ml (1 teaspoon) fresh ginger, pulped
5ml (1 teaspoon) fresh garlic, pulped
10ml (2 teaspoons) chilli powder
5ml (1 teaspoon) salt
2.5ml (½ teaspoon) turmeric
2 green chillis, chopped
fresh coriander leaves, chopped
300ml (½ pint) water
1kg (2lb) cod
300ml (½ pint) oil
GARNISH
   2 lemons, cut into wedges
   6 green chillis, slit down the middle

In a large bowl mix together the gram flour with all the spices, the green chillis and the coriander leaves. Stir in the water to form a semi-thick batter. Set aside. Cut the cod into about 8 pieces. Heat the oil in a heavy frying-pan. Dip the pieces of cod into the batter and fry over a medium heat, turning once. Arrange on a shallow, oval-shaped dish and garnish with lemon wedges and slit green chillis.

Jhingay aur saag
PRAWNS WITH SPINACH

This is an attractive dish to serve as an accompaniment, especially at parties, and will also freeze well.

SERVES 4–6
225 g (8 oz) frozen prawns
350 g (14 oz) canned spinach purée or frozen
spinach, thawed and chopped
2 tomatoes
150 ml ($\frac{1}{4}$ pint) oil
2.5 ml ($\frac{1}{2}$ teaspoon) mustard seeds
2.5 ml ($\frac{1}{2}$ teaspoon) onion seeds
5 ml (1 teaspoon) fresh ginger, pulped
5 ml (1 teaspoon) fresh garlic, pulped
5 ml (1 teaspoon) chilli powder
5 ml (1 teaspoon) salt

Thaw the prawns and leave in a bowl of cold water. Drain the can of spinach. Slice the tomatoes. Heat the oil and add the mustard and onion seeds. Lower the heat, add the tomatoes, spinach, all the spices and salt and stir-fry (using the *bhoono*-ing method) for about 5–7 minutes. Drain all the water off the prawns and add these to the spinach. Stir the prawns gently to mix, cover and simmer over a low heat for about 7–10 minutes.

Opposite *A meal of carefully balanced colours and textures, with* shaami *(meat – in this case lamb) kebabs, tandoori prawns and lamb biryani.*

Overleaf, left Chaplee kebabs *(minced lamb kebabs with pomegranate seeds), a refreshing* kachoomer *(onions and tomatoes in lemon juice) and* dahi ki kadi *(dumplings in yoghurt).*

Overleaf, right *A simple meal for an informal dinner party: plain boiled rice* (khushka) *and* chapatis, kheema matar *(mince with peas) and* bhindi bhujia *(okra curry) with* khatti dhaal *(lemon lentils).*

Tamatar jhingay
PRAWNS WITH TOMATOES

SERVES 4–6
3 medium onions
1 green pepper
5 ml (1 teaspoon) fresh ginger, pulped
5 ml (1 teaspoon) fresh garlic, pulped
5 ml (1 teaspoon) salt
5 ml (1 teaspoon) chilli powder
30 ml (2 tablespoons) lemon juice
350 g (12 oz) frozen prawns
45 ml (3 tablespoons) oil
400 g (14 oz) canned tomatoes
fresh coriander leaves to decorate

Peel and slice the onions. Slice the green pepper. In a small bowl weigh out all the spices, add the lemon juice and mix to a paste. Soak the prawns in cold water.

Heat the oil in a medium-sized saucepan, add the onions and fry until golden brown. Add all the spices, turn the heat low and mix well, stirring, for about 3 minutes. Add the can of tomatoes, with the juice, and the green pepper, and cook for 5–7 minutes. Add the prawns, after draining well, and cook for 10 minutes, stirring occasionally. Decorate with coriander leaves.

Serve hot with plain boiled rice and a crisp green salad.

Opposite *The hot north Indian dish* nehari *is a meal in itself. It is shown here with a plate of trimmings (shredded ginger, coriander, onion and chilli) and* naan.

Thalay huway jhingay aur mirch
FRIED PRAWNS WITH PEPPERS

This is a colourful and impressive side dish for a dinner party. As there are not many spices in this recipe I like to use a lot of fresh coriander in it.

SERVES 4
450 g (1 lb) prawns
5 ml (1 teaspoon) fresh garlic, pulped
5 ml (1 teaspoon) salt
½ bunch fresh coriander leaves, chopped finely
1 medium green pepper, sliced
1 medium red pepper, sliced
75 g (3 oz) unsalted butter

Thaw the prawns and rinse under a cold tap twice. Add the garlic, salt and fresh coriander leaves and leave aside. Slice the green and red peppers. In a large frying-pan melt the butter, add the prawns and stir-fry, tossing the prawns gently for 10–12 minutes. Add the peppers and fry for a further 3–5 minutes. Serve hot.

Sookhay jhingay
DRIED PRAWNS

This is a more economical way of cooking prawns. You can buy the dried prawns in packets from most Indian and Pakistani grocers.

SERVES 4
200 g (8 oz) dried prawns
2 medium onions
3 green chillis
fresh coriander leaves
300 ml (½ pint) oil
7.5 ml (1½ teaspoons) fresh ginger, pulped
7.5 ml (1½ teaspoons) fresh garlic, pulped
pinch turmeric
5 ml (1 teaspoon) salt
5 ml (1 teaspoon) chilli powder
30 ml (2 tablespoons) lemon juice

Soak the prawns in cold water for about 2 hours. Drain the water and wash twice. Slice the onions, chop the green chillis and fresh coriander leaves. In a large saucepan heat 150 ml (¼ pint) oil and fry the sliced onions along with 2 green chillis and half of the fresh coriander leaves. Stir-fry until golden brown. Add the ginger, garlic, turmeric, salt and chilli powder and stir-fry for a further 2 minutes over a low heat. Turn the heat off and leave aside.

In a separate saucepan heat the remaining oil and fry the prawns until crisp. When all the prawns are fried add to the onions and blend together. Return to the heat and stir-fry for a further 3–5 minutes.

Serve with *chapati*.

Tandoori jhingay
TANDOORI-STYLE PRAWNS

These mouth-watering prawns can be served as a starter arranged on a bed of lettuce with a lemon wedge, or as an attractive side dish for almost any meal. Though not essential, it is best to shell the prawns before cooking them as some people find it a bit awkward to shell them at the table.

SERVES 4
10–12 king prawns, shelled
100 g (4 oz) unsalted butter
5 ml (1 teaspoon) fresh ginger, pulped
5 ml (1 teaspoon) fresh garlic, pulped
5 ml (1 teaspoon) chilli powder
2.5 ml ($\frac{1}{2}$ teaspoon) salt
5 ml (1 teaspoon) ground coriander
5 ml (1 teaspoon) ground cumin
fresh coriander leaves, finely chopped
a few drops red colouring
GARNISH
   8 lettuce leaves
   1 small onion, cut into rings
   1–2 green chillis, chopped
   1 lemon, cut into wedges

Shell and wash the prawns. Place on a heatproof dish. Melt the butter and add all the spices including the coriander leaves and the colouring. Brush the melted butter mixture on the prawns and place them under a very hot pre-heated grill for 10–12 minutes, turning once. Serve on a bed of lettuce with onion rings, finely chopped green chilli and lemon wedges.

CHAPTER 11
Rice (chawal)

Rice is served with almost every meal in India, so the Indians have created a variety of ways of cooking it, each quite distinctive. As plain boiled rice is eaten by most people every day, for entertaining we tend to choose a more interesting rice dish, such as *pulao* (which has different-coloured grains and spices in it) or a biryani dish, in which rice is cooked with meat or chicken as well as spices.

Whatever the dish, the aim is to produce dry, separate-grained rice that is cooked through yet still has some 'bite' to it. The secret is to be reasonably precise about the amount of water you add to the rice, so that the rice can absorb all of it.

For biryanis it is best to half-cook the rice before adding the meat. There are two ways of doing this: one is the way I describe in my recipes (boiling the rice, water and whole spices together); the other is to boil the water first and then add the rice to it. When the rice is half-cooked, drain it well. Personally I find the first method easier.

Basmati rice, a long-grained milled white rice grown in both India and Pakistan, is the type I recommend, because it cooks very well and gives an excellent finished result. It is best to soak it for about 20–30 minutes before cooking, to prevent the grains from sticking to one another, but time does not always allow for this. Always make sure you use a tight-fitting lid for your rice saucepan. If you do not have one that fits tightly enough, either wrap a tea-cloth round the lid or put some tinfoil between the lid and the saucepan. Try not to remove the lid until the rice is cooked. (The advantage of using just a lid is that you can tell when the rice is ready because steam begins to escape, visibly and rapidly.)

Before serving, move the rice about gently with a slotted spoon to introduce air (the slotted spoon will prevent your breaking up the grains, which makes the rice mushy).

As a rough guide, though this does vary enormously according to individual appetite and the number of other dishes being served, allow about 75 g (3 oz) rice per person.

Rice can be cooked before your guests arrive and kept warm, covered, in a low oven (or can be re-heated over a low heat) until you are ready to turn it out on to its serving dish, which should ideally be a flat, oval-shaped one.

Khushka
PLAIN BOILED RICE

One good thing about plain boiled rice is that it can be served with almost anything. It should be well washed so that it is brilliant white when served.

SERVES 4
500g (1 lb) basmati rice
5 ml (1 teaspoon) salt
750 ml (1¼ pints) water

Pick over and wash the rice thoroughly until the water runs clear. Place the rice in a saucepan (preferably a heavy-bottomed one) and add the salt and the water. Bring to the boil, turn the heat very low and cover. Cook for 10–12 minutes.

Bagara khana
FRIED SPICY RICE

I use ginger and garlic for this beautifully aromatic rice dish, which give it a lovely flavour. If desired, you can add a few peas to it for extra colour and variety.

SERVES 4–6
450g (1 lb) rice
1 medium onion
30 ml (2 tablespoons) ghee
5 ml (1 teaspoon) fresh ginger, pulped
5 ml (1 teaspoon) fresh garlic, pulped
5 ml (1 teaspoon) salt
5 ml (1 teaspoon) black cumin seeds
3 whole cloves
3 whole green cardamoms
2 cinnamon sticks
4 peppercorns
750 ml (1¼ pints) water

Pick over and wash the rice. Peel and slice the onion. Melt the ghee in a large saucepan and fry the onion until a crisp golden brown. Add the ginger, garlic and salt. Turn off the heat. Remove half of the onion from the saucepan and leave aside. Return the saucepan to the heat, add the rice, black cumin seeds, cloves, cardamoms, cinnamon sticks and peppercorns and stir-fry for 3–5 minutes. Add the water, bring to the boil and lower the heat. Cover and cook until steam comes out through the lid. Check to see whether the rice is cooked. Transfer to a shallow oval-shaped dish and serve garnished with the fried onions.

Tamatar ka khana
TOMATO RICE

Rice cooked with tomatoes and onions will add colour to your table, especially when garnished with green chillis, coriander leaves and hard-boiled eggs. Serve this with any kebab dish and a *raita*.

SERVES 4
2 medium onions
150 ml (¼ pint) oil
5 ml (1 teaspoon) onion seeds
5 ml (1 teaspoon) fresh ginger, pulped
5 ml (1 teaspoon) fresh garlic, pulped
2.5 ml (½ teaspoon) turmeric
5 ml (1 teaspoon) chilli powder
7.5 ml (1½ teaspoons) salt
400 g (14 oz) canned tomatoes
500 g (1 lb) basmati rice
600 ml (1 pint) water
GARNISH
   3 green chillis
   fresh coriander leaves
   3 hard-boiled eggs

Peel and slice the onions. Heat the oil in a saucepan and fry the onions until golden brown. Add the onion seeds, ginger, garlic, turmeric, chilli powder and salt, lower the heat and add the canned tomatoes. Stir-fry for 10 minutes, breaking up the tomatoes. Wash the rice and add to the tomato mixture, stirring gently. Stir in the water, cover and cook over a low heat until the water has been absorbed and the rice is cooked. Transfer into a shallow oval-shaped dish and garnish with the green chillis, fresh coriander leaves and hard-boiled eggs.

Subzee pulao
VEGETABLE PULAO

This is a lovely way of cooking rice and vegetables together, and the saffron gives it a beautiful aroma. Serve this with a *raita* and any kebab dish.

SERVES 4–6

2 medium potatoes, each peeled and cut into 6
1 medium aubergine, cut into 6
200 g (8 oz) carrots, peeled and sliced
50 g (2 oz) beans, cut into pieces
60 ml (4 tablespoons) ghee
2 medium onions, sliced
175 ml (7 fl oz) yoghurt
10 ml (2 teaspoons) fresh ginger, pulped
10 ml (2 teaspoons) fresh garlic, pulped
10 ml (2 teaspoons) garam masala
10 ml (2 teaspoons) black cumin seeds
2.5 ml ($\frac{1}{2}$ teaspoon) turmeric
3 black cardamoms
2 cinnamon sticks
10 ml (2 teaspoons) salt
5 ml (1 teaspoon) chilli powder
600 g (1$\frac{1}{2}$ lb) basmati rice
300 ml ($\frac{1}{2}$ pint) milk
2.5 ml ($\frac{1}{2}$ teaspoon) saffron strands, boiled in
    300 ml ($\frac{1}{2}$ pint) milk
75 ml (5 tablespoons) lemon juice
GARNISH
    4 green chillis
    fresh coriander leaves

Wash and prepare all the vegetables. In a large frying-pan heat the ghee and fry all the vegetables. Remove from the pan and leave aside. Fry the sliced onions until soft and add the yoghurt, ginger, garlic, garam masala, 5 ml (1 teaspoon) black cumin seeds, turmeric, 1 cardamom, 1 cinnamon stick, 5 ml (1 teaspoon) salt and the chilli powder and stir-fry for 3–5 minutes. Add all the vegetables and fry for a further 4–5 minutes. Remove from the heat and set this mixture aside.

In a large saucepan half-cook the rice with 5 ml (1 teaspoon) salt, 2 cinnamon sticks, 2 black cardamoms and 5 ml (1 teaspoon) black cumin seeds. Drain, then leave half the rice in the pan while transferring the other half to a tray. Pour the vegetable mixture on top of the rice in the saucepan. Pour half the lemon juice and half of the saffron in milk over the vegetables and rice, cover with the remaining rice and pour the remaining lemon juice and saffron in milk sparingly on the top. Garnish with the chopped green chillis and chopped coriander leaves, return to the heat and cover tightly. Cook over a low heat for about 20 minutes. Check to see if the rice is cooked right through and mix before serving.

Kitcheri
SPICED RICE AND LENTILS

This is a lovely combination of rice and masoor dhaal, simple to cook and delicious served with minced lamb and *thill ki chutney*. When I serve *kitcheri* I like to add a knob of unsalted butter.

SERVES 4
200g (8oz) basmati rice
175g (6oz) masoor dhaal
30ml (2 tablespoons) pure or vegetable ghee
1 small onion, sliced
5ml (1 teaspoon) fresh ginger, pulped
5ml (1 teaspoon) fresh garlic, pulped
2.5ml ($\frac{1}{2}$ teaspoon) turmeric
600ml (1 pint) water
5ml (1 teaspoon) salt

Combine the rice and *dhaal* and wash, rubbing with your fingers, twice. Leave aside. In a large saucepan heat the ghee and add the sliced onion. Fry for 2 minutes. Lower the heat. Add the ginger, garlic and turmeric; stir-fry for another minute. Add the rice and blend together, mixing gently. Add the water, bring to the boil, lower the heat and cook, covered, for 20–25 minutes. Add salt and mix before serving.
Note Moong dhaal may be substituted for masoor dhaal in this recipe.

Opposite *Prawn* pulao *is the special rice dish in this picture, flanked by* tamatar ki chutney *(a tomato curry with hard-boiled eggs),* chicken kebabs *and an almond cake,* badaam ke lauze, *which is traditionally cut into diamond shapes. Water melon completes the meal.*

Overleaf, left *The popular lamb curry* roghan goshth *is accompanied by* tarka dhaal *(oil-dressed lentils garnished with green pepper), with vermicelli pudding (*sheer khorma*) to follow.*

Overleaf, right *This spread shows how attractive Indian snacks can look when displayed for an early-evening party. At the top is* upma *(savoury semolina); the drinks are hot, spicy tea, mango juice and lime juice, and next to the fruit juices are* pakoray *(vegetable dumplings); the silver dish in the middle is filled with* chewra *(flaked rice, nuts and raisins), and on its right are* dahi vadas *(soft dumplings in yoghurt) and fruit* chaat *(sweet and sour fruit salad);* namak paras *are the deep-fried diamond-shaped pastries on the left, with* gulab jamun *(deep-fried sweetmeat in syrup) next to them and* chohlay *(chick pea snack) centre front.*

Goshth ki biryani
LAMB BIRYANI

Cooked on festive occasions, especially for weddings, lamb biryani is amongst the most popular dishes in India. Served with a *raita*, it cannot fail to please. The meat can be cooked in advance and added to the rice on the day of the party, and the saffron gives it a beautiful aroma.

SERVES 4–6
150 ml ($\frac{1}{4}$ pint) milk
5 ml (1 teaspoon) saffron
60 ml (4 tablespoons) lemon juice
2 green chillis
$\frac{1}{4}$ bunch fresh coriander leaves
3 medium onions
75 ml (5 tablespoons) ghee
1 kg (2 lb) lean lamb, cubed
105 ml (7 tablespoons) natural yoghurt
7.5 ml (1$\frac{1}{2}$ teaspoons) fresh ginger, pulped
7.5 ml (1$\frac{1}{2}$ teaspoons) fresh garlic, pulped
10 ml (2 teaspoons) garam masala
10 ml (2 teaspoons) salt
1 pinch ($\frac{1}{4}$ teaspoon) turmeric
500 g (1 lb) basmati rice
10 ml (2 teaspoons) black cumin seeds
3 cardamoms

Boil the 150 ml ($\frac{1}{4}$ pint) milk with the saffron and leave aside with the lemon juice, green chillis and fresh coriander leaves. Slice the onions and fry in ghee in a large saucepan until golden brown. Remove half the onions and ghee from the saucepan, place in a bowl and leave aside with the saffron and other ingredients.

Combine together the meat, yoghurt, ginger, garlic, garam masala, 5 ml (1 teaspoon) salt and turmeric in a large bowl and mix well. Return the saucepan with the ghee and fried onions to the heat, add the meat mixture, stir for about 3 minutes and add 600 ml (1 pint) water. Leave over a low heat for 45 minutes, stirring occasionally. Check to see whether the meat is tender: if not, add 150 ml ($\frac{1}{4}$ pint) water and cook for a further 15 minutes. Once all the water has evaporated, stir-fry for about 2 minutes and leave aside.

Meanwhile, wash the rice, add the cumin seeds, cardamoms, salt and sufficient water for cooking, and cook over a medium heat until the rice is half-cooked. Remove from the heat and drain. Place half the rice in a tray and leave the other half in the large saucepan. Put the cooked meat on top of the rice (in the saucepan), half of all the ingredients (saffron-flavoured milk, lemon juice, etc.) on the meat and the other half of the rice on top and the remaining ingredients on the tray. Cover tightly with a lid and cook over a low heat for 15–20 minutes or until the rice is cooked.

Opposite *In the* karahi *at the top of this shot is* karahi murgh *(chicken), with* khichra *(lamb and lentils) in the centre; the sweet rice dish* zarda, *topped with* varq, *is at the front.*

Kuchchi yukhni ki murgh biryani
CHICKEN BIRYANI

This biryani recipe may look rather complicated, but is not difficult to follow. You can substitute lamb for chicken but you would have to marinate it overnight. As lamb takes a little longer to cook, make sure you increase the cooking time as well. This dish is another one from Hyderabad and, like all biryanis, is considered special because it contains saffron.

SERVES 6
7.5 ml (1½ teaspoons) fresh ginger, pulped
7.5 ml (1½ teaspoons) fresh garlic, pulped
15 ml (1 tablespoon) garam masala
5 ml (1 teaspoon) chilli powder
2.5 ml (½ teaspoon) turmeric
10 ml (2 teaspoons) salt
20 crushed green/white cardamom seeds
300 ml (10 fl oz) natural yoghurt
1.5 kg (3 lb) chicken, skinned and cut into 8
150 ml (¼ pint) milk
5 ml (1 teaspoon) saffron strands
4 green chillis
fresh coriander leaves
60 ml (4 tablespoons) lemon juice
90 ml (6 tablespoons) ghee
2 medium onions, sliced
500 g (1 lb) basmati rice
2 cinnamon sticks
4 peppercorns
5 ml (1 teaspoon) black cumin seeds

Blend together the ginger, garlic, garam masala, chilli powder, turmeric, 5 ml (1 teaspoon) of the salt and crushed cardamom seeds and mix with the yoghurt and chicken pieces. Leave aside for at least 3 hours at room temperature. Meanwhile, boil the milk, pour over the saffron in a bowl and leave aside on a large tray. Chop the green chillis and coriander leaves finely and leave on a small plate together with the saffron and milk on the tray. Leave the lemon juice on the same tray as well. In a separate large saucepan heat the ghee and fry the onions until golden brown. Remove half the onions and ghee from the saucepan and leave aside along with the other ingredients. Wash the rice about 3 times, add twice as much water, the cinnamon sticks, 4 peppercorns and the black cumin seeds. Bring the rice to the boil and remove from the heat when half-cooked (when you rub the grains between your finger and thumb the outside will be soft while the inside is still hard). Drain thoroughly and pour the rice on to a tray. Add the remaining 5 ml (1 teaspoon) salt to the rice. Put the chicken mixture into the saucepan with half the onions and ghee. Start pouring half the ingredients on the tray on to the chicken. Starting with half the green chillis and the coriander leaves, pour half the lemon juice and half the saffron. Pour the rice over this and then the rest of the ingredients on the tray, including the fried onions and ghee. Cover the saucepan tightly with a lid so no steam escapes (wrap the lid in a clean tea-towel if necessary). Cook on a low heat for about 1 hour. Check that the meat is cooked right through before serving. If the meat is not cooked, return to the heat and cook for a further 15 minutes. Mix with a perforated spoon before serving.

Pulao
PULAO RICE

SERVES 2–4
200 g (8 oz) basmati rice
30 ml (2 tablespoons) ghee
3 green cardamoms
2 cloves
3 peppercorns
2.5 ml ($\frac{1}{2}$ teaspoon) salt
2.5 ml ($\frac{1}{2}$ teaspoon) saffron
400 ml ($\frac{3}{4}$ pint) water
5 ml (1 teaspoon) kevra *water (see glossary)*

Wash the rice twice and leave aside. Heat the ghee in a saucepan. Add the cardamoms, cloves and peppercorns and fry for about 1 minute. Add the rice and stir-fry for a further 2 minutes. Add the salt, saffron and water and lower the heat. Cover and simmer over a low heat until the water has evaporated. Sprinkle the *kevra* water over the top.

Jhingay ka pulao
PRAWN PULAO

This recipe features caraway seeds, which give a distinctive taste and aroma to this unusual prawn *pulao*. Serve with a *raita* and *shaami* kebabs.

SERVES 4
450 g (1 lb) frozen prawns
5 ml (1 teaspoon) chilli powder
7.5 ml (1½ teaspoons) caraway seeds
2 cinnamon sticks
2 green cardamoms
2 bay leaves
5 ml (1 teaspoon) fresh ginger, pulped
5 ml (1 teaspoon) salt
2 medium onions
2.5 ml (¼ teaspoon) saffron
150 ml (¼ pint) milk
450 g (1 lb) basmati rice
75 ml (5 tablespoons) ghee
60 ml (4 tablespoons) lemon juice
mint leaves

Thaw the prawns out by putting them in a bowl of cold water. Prepare all the spices. Chop the onions. Prepare the saffron by boiling 150 ml (¼ pint) milk and adding the saffron. Leave aside. Grind to a fine paste the chilli powder, 5 ml (1 teaspoon) caraway seeds, the cinnamon sticks, green cardamoms, 1 sliced onion, the bay leaves and ginger. Leave aside.

In a separate saucepan wash the rice and when the rice is half-cooked remove from the heat and leave aside. Heat the ghee in a saucepan and fry the remaining onion until golden brown. Leave aside on a tray with the lemon juice and mint leaves.

Add the paste of spices and prawns to the ghee and stir-fry for about 5 minutes. Remove the prawns and spices and place on a separate dish. Arrange the half-cooked rice in the saucepan and pour the prawn mixture over. Pour half the lemon juice, half the onions and half the saffron over of the prawns. Arrange the other half of the rice on top and pour over the remaining ingredients. Garnish with the mint leaves, cover and cook over a low heat for 15–20 minutes. Mix before serving. Serve on a shallow oval-shaped dish.

Khabooli
CHANA DHAAL COOKED WITH RICE

I use saffron for this dish, which makes it rather special. It is delicious served with any *raita* and a meat curry such as *maya khalia* (spicy lamb curry).

SERVES 6
100g (4oz) chana dhaal
2 medium onions
60ml (4 tablespoons) ghee
5ml (1 teaspoon) fresh ginger, pulped
5ml (1 teaspoon) fresh garlic, pulped
2.5ml (½ teaspoon) turmeric
10ml (2 teaspoons) salt
2.5ml (½ teaspoon) chilli powder
5ml (1 teaspoon) garam masala
75ml (5 tablespoons) yoghurt
1.35 litres (2¼ pints) water
150ml (¼ pint) milk
5ml (1 teaspoon) saffron
45ml (3 tablespoons) lemon juice
2 green chillis
fresh coriander leaves
3 black cardamoms
3 black cumin seeds
500g (1 lb) basmati rice

Wash and soak the chana dhaal for 3 hours. Peel and slice the onions. Wash and pick over the rice and leave aside. Heat the ghee and fry the onion until golden brown. Remove half of the onion with a little of the ghee and set aside in a bowl. Add the ginger, garlic, turmeric, 5 ml (1 teaspoon) of the salt, the chilli powder and garam masala and stir-fry for 5 minutes. Stir in the yoghurt and add the chana dhaal and 150 ml (¼ pint) water and cook, covered, for 15 minutes. Remove from the heat and set aside. Meanwhile, boil the milk with the saffron and leave aside with the fried onion, lemon juice, green chillis and fresh coriander leaves. Boil the rest of the water and add the salt, black cardamoms, black cumin seeds and the rice, and cook, stirring occasionally, until the rice is half-cooked. Drain completely, leave half the rice in the pan and place the other half on a tray. Place the chana dhaal mixture and half of the fried onion, saffron, lemon juice, green chillis and fresh coriander leaves on top of the chana dhaal mixture. Place the remaining rice on top of this and the rest of the fried onion, saffron, lemon juice, chillis and coriander on top of the rice. Cover tightly with a lid and cook for about 20 minutes over a very low heat. Mix with a slotted spoon before serving.

CHAPTER 12
Breads (roti)

The most common Indian breads are *chapati, parata* and *poori,* all of which can be made with wholemeal flour – so they are very healthy foods. These three breads, in particular, are cooked almost every day in most Indian households. Another very popular bread, *naan,* is not usually prepared at home because ideally it should be made in a *tandoor,* or clay oven, and these are found only in restaurants. Most Indian people buy *naans* from their nearest restaurant, but I cook mine at home under a very hot pre-heated grill. The recipe is easy to follow and when cooked the *naans* are wonderfully soft and have a beautiful smell.

As well as these breads you will find in this section *roghni roti* (a lightly fried bread), stuffed *parata* and *besun ki roti* (gram flour bread). All of these freeze well.

Indian breads are made as individual portions, and I suggest you allow two per person. If you have frozen them, re-heat them either under a grill or in the oven (a microwave is useful for this); traditionally, of course, you would use a *thawa.* However, for parties there is nothing like freshly made bread, and if time allows the ideal would be to make it about two hours before.

Parata
LAYERED BREAD

The dough for *parata* is made in the same way and in the same quantities as those used for *chapati* but will make half the number of breads as *paratas* are thicker and a little larger when rolled out. Thinner than *naan* when cooked, *paratas* are fried rather than grilled or baked.

MAKES 8
225 g (8 oz) wholemeal flour (ata or chapati flour)
2.5 ml (½ teaspoon) salt
200 ml (⅓ pint) water
100 g (4 oz) pure or vegetable ghee

Divide the dough into 6–8 portions. Roll out each on a floured surface. Brush the middle with about 2.5 ml (½ teaspoon) ghee. Fold in half, roll (manually) into a pipe-like shape, flatten with your palms, then roll round your finger to form a coil. Roll out again using flour to dust as and when necessary. Roll out again to about 18 cm (7 inches) diameter.

Heat a heavy-bottomed frying-pan or *thawa* and slap the *parata* on to this. Move it around in the pan to ensure an even exposure to the heat. Turn over and brush with about 5 ml (1 teaspoon) of the ghee. Cook, then turn over once again and cook, still moving it around, for about 30 seconds. Remove from the heat and serve warm.

Stuffed parata
PARATA STUFFED WITH VEGETABLES

This bread can be quite rich and is usually made for special occasions. It can be eaten on its own or with any meat or vegetable curry. You may use cauliflower or grated radish (English or white – mooli) instead of the potato filling.

MAKES 4–6
FILLING
    3 medium potatoes
    2.5 ml (½ teaspoon) turmeric
    5 ml (1 teaspoon) garam masala
    5 ml (1 teaspoon) fresh ginger, pulped
    fresh coriander leaves
    3 green chillis
    5 ml (1 teaspoon) salt
DOUGH
    225 g (8 oz) wholemeal flour (ata or chapati flour)
    2.5 ml (½ teaspoon) salt
    200 ml (⅓ pint) water
    100 g (4 oz) pure or vegetable ghee
30 ml (2 tablespoons) ghee

Wash, peel and boil the potatoes until soft enough to be mashed. Blend in all the spices including the coriander leaves, finely chopped green chillis and salt. Mix together and set aside.

Make the dough according to the *parata* recipe above. Divide the dough into 6–8 equal portions. Roll each out on a floured surface. Spread about 15 ml (1 tablespoon) of the mashed potato mixture on each and cover with another rolled-out piece. Seal the edges well. Heat a heavy-bottomed frying-pan or a *thawa* and slap the *parata* gently on to it. Turn over and fry in 10 ml (2 teaspoons) ghee, turning and moving it about gently with a flat spoon. Remove from the pan and serve immediately. These *paratas* can be kept warm covered in tinfoil.

Besun ki roti
GRAM FLOUR BREAD

This filling *roti* is not eaten on a regular basis but is cooked occasionally. It is best served with the white radish curry *mooli ki bhujia,* but goes well with any vegetarian curry and lime pickle. Allow two pieces per person.

SERVES 2–3; MAKES 4–6
100g (4oz) wholemeal flour (ata or chapati flour)
75g (3oz) gram flour
2.5ml (½ teaspoon) salt
1 small onion
fresh coriander
2 green chillis
150ml (¼ pint) water
10ml (2 teaspoons) ghee

Sift the wholemeal and gram flours together into a large bowl. Add the salt. Chop the onion, fresh coriander and green chillis very finely. Blend into the flour mixture and add the water to form a soft dough. Cover and leave aside for 15 minutes. Knead for 5–7 minutes. Divide into 8 equal portions. Roll out to about 18cm (7 inches) on a lightly floured surface and cook over a medium heat in a frying-pan (or *thawa*), turning three times and lightly greasing each side with the ghee. Serve hot.

Roghni roti
LIGHTLY FRIED BREAD

This is rather a rich *roti,* made only occasionally. Served with egg curry (*khageena*) or ground almonds in ghee and milk (*badaam ka hareera*), it is delicious. Allow two *roti* per person.

SERVES 5; MAKES 10
225g (8oz) wholemeal flour (ata or chapati flour)
2.5ml (½ teaspoon) salt
15ml (1 tablespoon) ghee
300ml (½ pint) water

Place the wholemeal flour and the salt in a large mixing bowl. Make a well in the middle, add the ghee and rub in well. Gradually stir in the water. Work to a soft dough. Set aside for 10–15 minutes. Knead for 5–7 minutes. Divide into about 10 equal portions. Roll out like a pancake on a lightly floured surface. Using a sharp knife, lightly draw lines in a criss-cross pattern on each *roti.* Heat a heavy-bottomed frying-pan or a *thawa* and gently slap the *roti* on to it. Turn it over after about 1 minute and rub on 5ml (1 teaspoon) of ghee; turn over again and fry, moving it about with a spatula. Turn over once more, remove from the pan and serve hot.

Opposite Kitcheri *(rice and lentils) is shown here with poppadums, egg curry* (khageena) *and, on the left,* thill ki chutney *(sesame seed chutney).*

Naan
YEASTED BREAD

There are many ways of making *naans*, but this particular recipe is very easy to follow. *Naans* should be served warm, preferably immediately after cooking.

MAKES 6–8
5 ml (1 teaspoon) sugar
5 ml (1 teaspoon) fresh yeast
150 ml (5 oz) warm water
200 g (8 oz) plain flour
15 ml (1 tablespoon) ghee
5 ml (1 teaspoon) salt
50 g (2 oz) unsalted butter
5 ml (1 teaspoon) poppy seeds

Put the sugar and the yeast in a cup with the warm water, mix well until the yeast has dissolved and leave aside for 10 minutes or until the mixture is frothy. Place the flour in a large mixing bowl, make a well in the middle, add the ghee and salt and pour in the yeast mixture. Mix well, using your hands and adding more water if required. Turn on to a floured surface and knead for about 5 minutes or until smooth. Place the dough back in the bowl, cover and leave to rise in a warm place for 1½ hours or until doubled in size. Turn on to a floured surface and knead for a further 2 minutes. Break off small balls with your hand and pat into rounds about 12 cm (5 inches) in diameter and 1 cm (½ inch) thick. Place on a greased sheet of tinfoil and grill under a very hot pre-heated grill for 7–10 minutes, turning twice to brush with butter and sprinkle with poppy seeds. Serve warm immediately, or keep wrapped in tinfoil until required.

Opposite *Shown here are all the ingredients for* khichra *(the finished dish can be seen opposite page 105): spices, meat, lemon, fresh garlic and ginger, onion, yoghurt, chillis and four types of lentil (from left to right they are chana dhaal, masoor dhaal, moong dhaal and urid dhaal).*

Chapati
UNLEAVENED BREAD

This is one of the less fattening Indian breads because it contains no fat, but some people like to brush it with a little melted butter before serving. Ideally *chapatis* should be eaten as they come off the *thawa*, or out of the frying-pan, but if that is not practical keep them warm after cooking by wrapping them up in foil. In India *chapatis* are sometimes cooked on a naked flame, which makes them puff up. Allow about 2 per person.

225g (8oz) wholemeal flour (ata or chapati flour)
2.5ml (½ teaspoon) salt
200ml (⅓ pint) water

Place the flour in a mixing bowl with the salt. Make a well in the middle and gradually stir in the water, mixing well with your fingers. Form a supple dough. Knead for about 7–10 minutes. Ideally, leave aside for about 15–20 minutes but if time is short roll out straight away. Divide into 10–12 equal portions. Roll out each piece on a well-floured surface. Have some foil ready to wrap the cooked *chapatis* in to keep them warm. Place a heavy-based frying-pan (or a *thawa*) on a high heat. When steam rises from it, lower the heat to medium, place a *chapati* in the pan and when it bubbles turn it over. Press down with a clean tea-cloth or a flat spoon and turn once again. Remove from the pan and keep warm. Repeat the process until all the *chapatis* are cooked. (Do not get disheartened if you are not successful the first time: you will improve with practice.)

Poori
DEEP-FRIED BREAD PUFFS

This bread is served mostly with vegetarian meals and particularly with potato curry (*aloo ki bhujia*) and semolina (*sooji ka halva*). Though *pooris* are deep-fried, they are very light. You can either pile them one on top of the other or leave them on a tray so that they remain puffed up. Allow two per person.

SERVES 5; MAKES 10
225g (8oz) wholemeal flour (ata or chapati flour)
2.5ml (½ teaspoon) salt
150ml (¼ pint) water
600ml (1 pint) oil

Place the wholemeal flour and salt in a bowl. Make a well in the middle, add the water gradually and work into a dough. Add more water if needed. Knead until smooth and elastic and set aside for about 15 minutes. Divide the dough into about 10 equal portions and with lightly oiled or floured hands pat each into a smooth ball. Roll out each ball on a lightly oiled or floured surface into a thin circle. Heat the oil in a deep-frying pan or *karahi* and deep-fry the *pooris*, turning once, until golden in colour. Drain well and remove from the pan. Serve immediately if possible; otherwise, keep warm wrapped in tinfoil.

CHAPTER 13

Accompaniments

Accompaniments — a simple carrot salad, a tangy lime pickle or a mint *raita* for example — always add colour and variety to a meal. Most take very little time to prepare but can make an ordinary meal memorable, especially if you are entertaining.

   None of these accompaniments has to be made in large quantities, because they are only taken in small amounts: variety is better than quantity, and it is worth giving some thought to the appearance and texture of the different items you are serving.

Lime pickle

A good, tangy pickle can be served at any meal. This lime pickle is easy to make but takes a considerable time to prepare.

10 limes
3 green chillis
45 ml (3 tablespoons) salt
300 ml ($\frac{1}{2}$ pint) oil
15 ml (1 tablespoon) mixed onion and mustard seeds
5 ml (1 teaspoon) white cumin seeds
4 dried red chillis
4 curry leaves
20 ml (1$\frac{1}{2}$ tablespoons) ground coriander
20 ml (1$\frac{1}{2}$ tablespoons) ground cumin
10 ml (2 teaspoons) chilli powder

Wash the limes, pat dry with kitchen paper and cut into quarters. Remove the pips. Slit the chillis and leave aside. Arrange the lime quarters and the green chillis in a pickling jar. Sprinkle the salt over the limes and chillis. Cover the mouth of the jar tightly and give it a shake. Leave the jar on a windowsill for about 3 weeks or until the limes are discoloured, shaking the jar once a day.

   Heat the oil in a saucepan and fry the mixed onion and mustard seeds, dried red chillis and curry leaves. Remove from the heat, add the ground coriander, ground cumin and chilli powder, stir and mix together. Return to the heat, add the limes and chillis to the pan and stir-fry for 2 minutes. Remove from the heat and leave to cool. Place in a large jar and leave for 2 hours. The pickle is now ready to be served.

Mint raita
YOGHURT SAUCE WITH MINT

Raitas are very easy to prepare, very versatile and have a cooling effect which will be appreciated if you are serving hot, spicy dishes.

200 ml (7 fl oz) natural yoghurt
50 ml (2 fl oz) water
1 small onion, finely chopped
2.5 ml (½ teaspoon) mint sauce
2.5 ml spoon (½ teaspoon) salt
3 mint leaves to garnish

Whip the yoghurt with a fork, gradually adding the water. Add the chopped onion, mint sauce and salt and blend together. Decorate with the mint leaves.

Kheeray ka raita
CUCUMBER RAITA

One of the most popular *raitas* of all, this makes an excellent accompaniment to almost any dish.

225 g (8 oz) cucumber
1 medium onion
2.5 ml (½ teaspoon) salt
2.5 ml (½ teaspoon) mint sauce
275 ml (10 fl oz) yoghurt
150 ml (¼ pint) water
mint leaves to garnish

Peel and slice the cucumber. Chop the onion finely. Place these in a liquidizer, then add the salt and the mint sauce. Finally, add the yoghurt and the water and blend well. Transfer to a serving bowl. Serve garnished with a few mint leaves.

Baingun raita
AUBERGINE RAITA

Virtually a 'must' at an Indian-style dinner party, *raitas* go well with anything and everything; what is more, they can always be made a day in advance.

SERVES 4
1 medium aubergine
5 ml (1 teaspoon) salt
1 small onion, finely chopped
2 green chillis, finely chopped
200 ml (7 fl oz) natural yoghurt
45 ml (3 tablespoons) water

Wash the aubergine and remove the top end. Discard the top and chop the rest into small pieces. Boil until soft and mushy. Drain and mash, then add the salt, the finely chopped onion and the chopped green chillis. Whip the yoghurt with the water and pour over the aubergine mixture. Mix well and serve.

Masalay dar corn
SPICY CORN

200 g (8 oz) canned or frozen sweetcorn
1 medium onion
5 ml (1 teaspoon) ground cumin
5 ml (1 teaspoon) fresh garlic, pulped
5 ml (1 teaspoon) ground coriander
5 ml (1 teaspoon) salt
2 green chillis
45 ml (3 tablespoons) unsalted butter
4 crushed red chillis
2.5 ml ($\frac{1}{2}$ teaspoon) lemon juice
fresh coriander leaves

Thaw or drain the corn (if using canned corn) and leave aside. Peel and finely chop the onion. Blend together in a food processor the ground cumin, garlic, ground coriander, salt, 1 green chilli and the finely chopped onion and grind to a paste.

Heat the butter in a frying-pan and add the onion mixture. Fry over a medium heat for 5–7 minutes. Add the crushed red chillis. Put in the corn and stir-fry for a further 2 minutes, then add the remaining green chilli, lemon juice and the fresh coriander leaves.

Serve hot as an accompaniment.

Hot salad

This quickly-made dish is ideal for a cold winter's night.

½ medium-sized cauliflower, cut into small florets
1 green pepper, sliced
1 red pepper, sliced
½ cucumber, sliced
4 carrots, peeled and sliced
30 ml (2 tablespoons) butter
salt and pepper to taste

Wash and prepare all the vegetables. Melt the butter, add all the vegetables and stir-fry for 5–7 minutes. Add the salt and pepper, cover with a lid, lower the heat and simmer for about 3 minutes. Remove from the heat and serve immediately.

Kheeray ki salad
COOL CUCUMBER SALAD

This cooling salad is another good foil for a highly spiced meal. Omit the green chilli if preferred.

225 g (8 oz) cucumber, peeled and sliced
1 green chilli (optional)
coriander leaves, finely chopped
30 ml (2 tablespoons) lemon juice
2.5 ml (½ teaspoon) salt
5 ml (1 teaspoon) sugar
mint leaves to decorate

Peel and slice the cucumber thinly and arrange on a round serving plate. Chop the green chilli and spread on top of the cucumber.

In a small bowl mix together the finely chopped coriander leaves, lemon juice, salt and sugar and leave aside. Chill the cucumber in the refrigerator for about 1 hour.

Pour the dressing over just before serving and decorate with a few mint leaves.

Thill ki chutney
SESAME SEED CHUTNEY

This chutney was always served with *khichra* (rice cooked with lentils) in our house in India, and the combination still appeals to me. I also use it to spread in sandwiches along with *shaami* kebabs for picnics.

120 ml (8 tablespoons) sesame seeds
30 ml (2 tablespoons) water
3 green chillis, chopped
½ bunch fresh coriander, chopped
5 ml (1 teaspoon) salt
10 ml (2 teaspoons) lemon juice
1 medium onion, cut into rings

Roast the sesame seeds and leave to cool. Put the sesame seeds in the food processor and grind to a fine powder. Add the water and mix to a paste. Put the green chillis and the fresh coriander in and grind again. Add the salt and lemon juice and grind once again. Remove from the food processor and place in a serving dish. Garnish with onion rings.

Dahi vale baingun
FRIED AUBERGINES IN YOGHURT

This makes a good alternative to a *raita*. The aubergines are fried until crisp, then given a *baghaar*, or seasoned oil dressing. The dish can be prepared in advance and does not need re-heating.

SERVES 4
200 ml (7 fl oz) natural yoghurt
75 ml (3 oz) water
5 ml (1 teaspoon) salt
1 medium aubergine
150 ml (¼ pint) oil
5 ml (1 teaspoon) white cumin seeds
6 dried red chillis

Whip the yoghurt with a fork, add the water and salt and mix well. Transfer into a serving dish. Slice the aubergine thinly. Heat the oil in a frying-pan and fry the sliced aubergine over a medium heat until it begins to turn crisp. Drop the fried aubergine slices into the yoghurt. When all have been fried, lower the heat, add the white cumin seeds and the dried red chillis and pour over the yoghurt and aubergines.

Fried corn & peas

This makes a colourful accompaniment to any meat or chicken dish – sprinkled over a dry chicken dish, such as spicy chicken, for example.

50 g (2 oz) unsalted butter
200 g (8 oz) frozen sweetcorn
200 g (8 oz) frozen peas
2.5 ml (½ teaspoon) salt
2.5 ml (½ teaspoon) chilli powder
15 ml (1 tablespoon) lemon juice
fresh coriander leaves to garnish

Melt the butter in a large saucepan. Add the corn and peas and fry, stirring occasionally, for about 10 minutes. Add the salt and chilli powder and fry for a further 5 minutes. Pour over the lemon juice. Serve garnished with fresh coriander leaves.

Imli ki chutney
TAMARIND CHUTNEY

A mouthwatering chutney which is extremely popular all over India, served with various vegetarian snacks. I enjoy this particularly with *pakoras* (dumplings) and *samosas*.

SERVES 4–6
30 ml (2 tablespoons) tamarind paste
75 ml (5 tablespoons) water
5 ml (1 teaspoon) chilli powder
2.5 ml (½ teaspoon) ground ginger
2.5 ml (½ teaspoon) salt
5 ml (1 teaspoon) sugar
chopped coriander leaves to garnish

Put the tamarind paste into a bowl and gradually add the water, gently whipping with a fork to form a smooth, runny paste. Add the chilli powder and the ginger and blend. Mix in the salt and the sugar and garnish with the finely chopped coriander leaves.

Kachoomer
ONIONS & TOMATOES IN LEMON JUICE

This will go with almost anything, and makes a good alternative to a salad.

1 medium onion
2 firm tomatoes
fresh coriander leaves
2 fresh green chillis
2.5 ml ($\frac{1}{2}$ teaspoon) salt
30 ml (2 tablespoons) lemon juice

Chop the onion, tomatoes, coriander leaves and green chillis finely. Add the salt and the lemon juice and mix.

If preparing a day in advance, omit the lemon juice and keep covered in the refrigerator. Add the lemon juice just before serving.

Kabli chana salad
CHICK PEA SALAD

This attractive-looking salad can be served with a couple of *shaami* kebabs for a delicious light luncheon or informal supper.

SERVES 4
400 g (15 oz) canned chick peas
4 carrots, peeled and sliced
1 bunch spring onions
1 medium cucumber
2.5 ml ($\frac{1}{2}$ teaspoon) salt
2.5 ml ($\frac{1}{2}$ teaspoon) coarsely ground black pepper
45 ml (3 tablespoons) lemon juice
1 red pepper, sliced

Drain the chick peas and place in a salad bowl. Peel and slice the carrots. Cut the spring onions into pieces and the cucumber into thick triangles. Place the carrots, spring onions and cucumber in the bowl of chick peas and mix together. Add the salt, pepper and lemon juice to the salad. Mix gently with a fork. Slice the red pepper thinly and lay the slices on top.

Gajar aur podinay ka salad
CARROT & MINT SALAD

This is a delightfully refreshing salad. Prepare it in advance and chill before serving.

SERVES 2–4
200g (8oz) carrots, grated
2.5ml ($\frac{1}{2}$ teaspoon) salt
5ml (1 teaspoon) mint sauce
mint leaves to garnish

Wash, peel and grate the carrots. Place in a serving dish. Add the salt and the mint sauce and blend. Chill for about 1 hour before serving. Garnish with a few mint leaves.

Aam ki chutney
MANGO CHUTNEY

Everyone's favourite chutney, this has a sweet and sour taste and is particularly good served with a mint *raita.* It is best made well in advance and stored for at least two weeks before use.

1kg (2lb) raw mangoes, peeled, halved and stoned
60ml (4 tablespoons) salt
600ml (1 pint) water
500g (1lb) sugar
450ml ($\frac{3}{4}$ pint) vinegar
10ml (2 teaspoons) fresh ginger, pulped
10ml (2 teaspoons) fresh garlic, pulped
10ml (2 teaspoons) chilli powder
2 cinnamon sticks
75g (3oz) raisins
100g (4oz) dates, stoned

Peel, halve and stone the mangoes. Cut into cubes, add the salt and water and leave overnight. Drain the liquid from the mangoes and leave aside. In a large saucepan bring the sugar and vinegar to the boil over a low heat. Add the mango cubes gradually, then all the spices, the raisins and the stoned dates, and bring to the boil again, stirring occasionally. Lower the heat and cook for about 1 hour or until the mixture thickens. Remove from the heat and leave to cool. Discard the cinnamon sticks. Spoon the chutney into clean dry jars and cover tightly with lids. Leave in a cool place for the flavour to develop.

Mooli ka raita
WHITE RADISH IN YOGHURT

This unusual combination of mooli (white radish) and yoghurt makes a good accompaniment to vegetarian curries. Like other *raitas*, it can be prepared in advance.

SERVES 4
6–8 mooli, thinly sliced
150 ml (7 fl oz) yoghurt
60 ml (4 tablespoons) water
5 ml (1 teaspoon) salt
2.5 ml (½ teaspoon) ground coriander
2.5 ml (½ teaspoon) chilli powder

Wash and trim the ends of the mooli. Slice thinly. Pour the yoghurt into a serving dish and stir in the water. Add the salt and the mooli to the yoghurt. Mix the ground coriander and chilli powder together and spread over the *raita*.

Paapar
POPPADUMS

Poppadums are crisp, wafer-thin crisps the size of a small pancake, made of pulses or dried rice and seasoned with black pepper or crushed red chillis. They are sold in Indian and Pakistani grocers.

There are three ways of cooking poppadums. The traditional method is by deep-frying, which helps to bring out the full flavour (poppadums are also very light when deep-fried). Once you have heated the oil in a deep-frying pan (or a *karahi*) drop the poppadum in and press down with a flat spoon as it begins to curl up (you have to fry them very quickly because they are very thin and will easily burn). Turn once and remove from the pan with a slotted spoon. If you find it difficult to fry poppadums whole, cut them into fours before frying.

The second method is to grill the poppadums, which cuts down the calories a little. All you do is place one on a grilling rack under a pre-heated grill. Watch it very carefully or it will burn. Turn it once. You will know it is cooked when a few bubbles begin to appear and the poppadum turns pale.

You can also cook poppadums by holding them, one at a time, of course, in some bacon tongs over a gas flame and moving them about.

Poppadums can be eaten either with meals or served with drinks. In restaurants they are often brought to the table before the meal is served so that diners have something to nibble before the food arrives.

CHAPTER 14

Snacks

In India, we like having tea parties at about 5 or 6 o'clock in the evening, especially in the month of Ramadan, when people meet after fasting all day, and we serve little snacks such as the ones in this section. The snacks in this chapter are ideal for cocktail or other drinks parties where you do not want to go to the trouble of providing a full-scale buffet but would like to offer something more interesting than the usual peanuts and crisps.

These snacks look good served in bowls or on small, attractive plates. Some can be eaten with the fingers but for others you will want to provide small plates, forks and sometimes spoons.

The basic quantities are for four people, which you can multiply according to the number on your guest list, but for some items, such as *chewra* (a popular rice-and-nut mixture), it is impossible to gauge the number.

Pakoray
DEEP-FRIED VEGETABLE DUMPLINGS

Pakoras are eaten all over India. They are made in many different ways and with a variety of fillings. Sometimes they are served in yoghurt. Our Nanny used to make these and the way she made them was the best I have ever tasted, so this is her recipe. *Pakoras* are the ideal hot snack for winter afternoons, especially served with an *imli ki chutney*.

90 ml (6 tablespoons) gram flour
2.5 ml (½ teaspoon) salt
5 ml (1 teaspoon) chilli powder
5 ml (1 teaspoon) baking powder
7.5 ml (1½ teaspoons) white cumin seeds
5 ml (1 teaspoon) pomegranate seeds
300 ml (½ pint) water
fresh coriander, finely chopped
oil for deep frying

Sift the gram flour into a large bowl. Add all the spices, baking powder, cumin and pomegranate seeds and blend together. Add the water and beat well together to form a smooth batter. Add the coriander. Leave aside.

Fill with any of the following: cauliflower cut into small florets, onions cut into rings, peeled and sliced potatoes, aubergines or fresh spinach leaves. Heat the oil in a heavy frying-pan or *karahi*, put in the vegetable of your choice and fry, turning once. Repeat the process until the batter is finished. Leave on kitchen paper to drain.

Samosas
DEEP-FRIED PASTIES

Samosas, which are a sort of Indian Cornish pasty, make excellent snacks. In India you can buy them along the roadside, and they are very popular. They are best made fresh but may be frozen and re-heated. The filling can be of either vegetable or meat. For a meat filling, use the recipe for *kheema matar* (minced lamb with peas, page 40). A vegetable filling is described below. With the *samosas* serve tomato ketchup with a little chilli powder in it.

MAKES 10–12

PASTRY

> 100 g (4 oz) self-raising flour
> 2.5 ml (½ teaspoon) salt
> 7.5 g (1½ oz) butter
> 60 ml (4 tablespoons) water

FILLING

> 3 medium potatoes, boiled
> 5 ml (1 teaspoon) fresh ginger, pulped
> 5 ml (1 teaspoon) fresh garlic, pulped
> 30 ml (2 tablespoons) lemon juice
> 2 small green chillis, finely chopped
> 2.5 ml (½ teaspoon) white cumin seeds
> 2.5 ml (½ teaspoon) onion and mustard seeds
> 5 ml (1 teaspoon) salt
> 2.5 ml (½ teaspoon) crushed red chillis

ghee or oil for deep frying

Sift the flour and salt in a bowl. Add the butter, cut into small pieces, and rub into the flour until the mixture resembles breadcrumbs. Pour in the water, mix with a fork, pat the dough into a ball and knead with the back of the hand for 5 minutes or until the dough is smooth. Add a little flour if the dough is sticky. Cover and leave aside.

For the filling, mash the boiled potatoes gently and add all the spices including the lemon juice and green chilli. Break small balls off the dough and roll out very thinly into a circle. Cut in half, dampen the edges and shape into cones. Fill the cones with a little of the filling, dampen the top and bottom edges of the cones and pinch together to seal. Set aside.

Fill a deep-frying pan one-third full with oil and heat until a small cube of stale bread turns golden in a few seconds when dropped into the oil. Carefully lower the *samosas* into the oil a few at a time and fry for 2–3 minutes or until golden brown. Remove from the oil and drain on kitchen towels.

Upma
SPICED SEMOLINA

A south Indian savoury snack which is very quick and easy to prepare, *upma* should be served warm. It has a lovely aroma, mainly from the curry leaves.

150 ml (¼ pint) oil
5 ml (1 teaspoon) mixed onion and mustard seeds
4 dried red chillis
4 curry leaves (fresh or dried)
50 g (2 oz) cashew nuts
120 ml (8 tablespoons) coarse semolina
5 ml (1 teaspoon) salt
150 ml (¼ pint) water

Heat the oil in a large, heavy frying-pan. Add the mixed seeds, dried red chillis and curry leaves and stir-fry for about 1 minute. Lower the heat and add the cashew nuts. Add the coarse semolina and quickly stir-fry, moving it all the time so that it does not burn. Stir-fry for about 5 minutes and add the salt. Add the water and cook, stirring continuously. Serve warm as a tea-time snack.

Masalay dar badaam
SPICED ALMONDS

Spiced almonds make a welcome change from peanuts and crisps to serve with drinks.

SERVES 4–6
200 g (8 oz) whole almonds
2.5 ml (½ teaspoon) chilli powder
2.5 ml (½ teaspoon) salt
2.5 ml (½ teaspoon) ground coriander

Soak the almonds in water for 3 hours. Drain and leave to dry on kitchen paper for about 30 minutes. Dry-roast the chilli powder, salt and ground coriander over a low heat in a saucepan. Add the almonds and roast, moving them about in the saucepan, for about 3–5 minutes. Remove from the heat and place in a serving dish.

Mayvay ka chaat
SWEET AND SOUR FRUIT

This fruit *chaat*, a mixture of fresh and canned fruit which has a sweet and sour flavour, is very cooling, especially in the summer. We would serve tea or fruit juices with this.

400 g (14 oz) canned mixed fruit cocktail
400 g (14 oz) canned guavas
2 large bananas
3 apples
5 ml (1 teaspoon) ground black pepper
5 ml (1 teaspoon) salt
30 ml (2 tablespoons) lemon juice
2.5 ml ($\frac{1}{2}$ teaspoon) ground ginger
mint leaves to garnish

Drain the fruit cocktail and place the fruit in a deep bowl. Mix the guavas and their syrup with the fruit cocktail. Peel the bananas and the apples. Dice the apples. Mix the fresh fruit and canned fruit and add the ground pepper, salt, lemon juice and ginger. Stir to mix. Serve as a snack garnished with a few mint leaves.

Indian-style omelette

I find omelettes very versatile: they go with almost anything and you can also serve them at any time of the day. For an informal lunch you could serve this with chips (I throw in a few bits of Cheddar cheese as well, though that is not a traditional touch!).

SERVES 2–4
1 small onion
2 green chillis
fresh coriander leaves
4 medium eggs
5 ml (1 teaspoon) salt
30 ml (2 tablespoons) oil

Peel and chop the onion very finely. Chop the green chillis and fresh coriander finely. Mix in a medium-sized bowl, ideally with your fingers. Whip the eggs in a separate bowl and add the onion mixture. Add the salt and whip together. Heat the oil in a large frying-pan, add 15 ml (1 tablespoon) of the oil and fry half the omelette, turning once and pressing down with a flat spoon to make sure the egg is cooked right through. Repeat the same process for the remaining ingredients. Serve immediately with *paratas* or toasted bread.

Namak paras
DEEP-FRIED DIAMOND PASTRIES

A simple-to-make snack which will retain its crispness if stored in an airtight container. Serve with drinks or at tea-time.

150 g (6 oz) plain flour
5 ml (1 teaspoon) baking powder
2.5 ml ($\frac{1}{2}$ teaspoon) salt
15 ml (1 tablespoon) black cumin seeds
100 ml (4 fl oz) water
300 ml ($\frac{1}{2}$ pint) oil

Place the flour, baking powder, salt and the black cumin seeds in a bowl and add water to form a soft, elasticated dough. Roll out on a clean surface to about 6 mm ($\frac{1}{4}$ inch) thick, then cut into diamond shapes, heat the oil until very hot and deep-fry until golden brown. Remove quickly, drain on kitchen paper and serve.

Chewra
MIXED FLAKED RICE, NUTS & RAISINS

This is one of the most popular nut mixtures in India and is very tasty. There are a number of ways of making this, but this is my favourite. I recommend that you make a large quantity and store it in an airtight container to serve with tea or alcoholic drinks.

50 g (2 oz) chana dhaal
300 ml ($\frac{1}{2}$ pint) oil
10 ml (2 teaspoons) onion seeds
6 curry leaves
200 g (8 oz) parva *(flaked rice)*
30 ml (2 tablespoons) peanuts
25 g (1 oz) raisins
75 g (3 oz) sugar
10 ml (2 teaspoons) salt
10 ml (2 teaspoons) chilli powder
50 g (2 oz) sev *(bought)*

Wash and soak the chana dhaal for at least 3 hours. Heat the oil in a saucepan and fry the onion seeds and the curry leaves. Add the flaked rice and fry until crisp and golden (do not allow to burn). Remove from the heat and place on kitchen paper on a small tray so that any excess oil is soaked up. Fry the peanuts in the remaining oil and mix with the flaked rice. Add the raisins, sugar, salt and chilli powder and mix together. Mix in the *sev*. Re-heat the oil remaining in the frying-pan and fry the soaked chana dhaal until golden. Add to the rest of the ingredients and mix together. This dish can be eaten straight away or stored in an airtight container until you need it.

Chohlay
CHICK PEA SNACK

Though you may use fresh chick peas (soaked overnight) for this very popular snack, eaten all over India, I find the canned sort quick and easy to use without sacrificing much flavour. There are many different ways of preparing this; my version features potatoes and tomatoes.

SERVES 2–4
400 g (14 oz) canned chick peas
2 medium potatoes
1 medium onion
30 ml (2 tablespoons) tamarind paste
90 ml (6 tablespoons) water
5 ml (1 teaspoon) chilli powder
10 ml (2 teaspoons) sugar
5 ml (1 teaspoon) salt
GARNISH
   1 tomato
   2 green chillis
   a few fresh coriander leaves

Open and drain the can of chick peas and transfer to a serving bowl. Peel and dice the potatoes, boil until cooked and leave aside. Peel and finely chop the onion. In a small bowl mix together the tamarind paste and water. Add the chilli powder, sugar and salt. Pour over the chick peas. Add the finely chopped onion and the diced potatoes. Taste and adjust the salt. Serve garnished with sliced tomatoes, chopped green chillis and fresh coriander leaves.

Dahi vadas
SOFT DUMPLINGS IN YOGHURT

Dahi vadas are very light and make a good summer afternoon snack as well as a good accompaniment to any vegetarian meal. They are usually served with their own special spice mixture (*masala*) in a small dish. They have a sweet and sour taste.

200g (8oz) urid dhaal powder
5ml (1 teaspoon) baking powder
2.5ml ($\frac{1}{2}$ teaspoon) ground ginger
oil for deep frying
400ml (15 fl oz) natural yoghurt
75g (3$\frac{1}{2}$oz) sugar

Place the powdered urid dhaal in a mixing bowl with the baking powder and ginger powder, add 300ml ($\frac{1}{2}$ pint) water and mix to form a paste. Heat the oil, preferably in a *karahi*, pour in the batter 5ml (1 teaspoon) at a time and deep-fry the *vadas* until golden brown, lowering the heat when the oil gets too hot. Leave the *vadas* aside. In a separate bowl mix the yoghurt, 400ml (15 fl oz) water and the sugar with a whisk or fork. Pour over the *vadas*.

Masala for dahi vadas

This *masala* (spice mixture) for the dumplings described above is usually made in a large quantity as it can be stored in an airtight container.

50g (2oz) coarsely ground coriander
50g (2oz) coarsely ground white cumin
75g (3oz) black salt
25g (1oz) crushed red chillis
100g (4oz) citric acid

Roast the coriander and the white cumin in a saucepan until a little darker in colour. Grind coarsely in a food processor. Add the black salt, crushed red chillis and citric acid and blend well together. Sprinkle about 15ml (1 tablespoon) of this masala all over the *dahi vadas* just before serving.

CHAPTER 15
Drinks

In India, owing to the hot climate, iced water is always served with meals, placed on the side in either a stainless steel or a pretty glass jug. You may wish to serve beer or lager when you cook Indian-style, but most people agree that wine is wasted with spicy food. As an alternative to alcohol or water I think fruit juice or any soft beverage goes down very well, and I have included a couple of fruit-based drinks in this short section. The famous Indian drink *lassi*, made with natural yoghurt, is another possibility. It is very refreshing and can be made with either salt or sugar – savoury or sweet – as desired.

For after the meal I have provided a spicy tea recipe which you might like to try instead of coffee.

Lassi
YOGHURT DRINK

This drink is wonderfully cooling. When I go back to India or Pakistan I make a point of stopping at a *lassi* shop. I particularly enjoy sweet *lassi*, but you may add salt instead of sugar if you prefer, for a savoury version.

SERVES 2
125 g (5 fl oz) yoghurt
45 ml (3 tablespoons) sugar or 15 ml
  (1 tablespoon) salt, to taste
300 ml (½ pint) water
150 ml (¼ pint) milk

It is best to make this drink in a liquidizer because whisking the yoghurt with a fork or hand-whisk will take at least 15 minutes. Whisk the yoghurt until frothy, add the sugar/salt and continue to whisk. Add the water and the milk and whisk for a further 5 minutes. Serve in long glasses with ice.

Aam ka phool
MANGO DRINK

For this recipe I use half-ripe mangoes, known as *kairis*, which are green.

SERVES 4
2 kairis
120–150 ml (8–10 tablespoons) sugar
600 ml (1 pint) milk

Boil the *kairis* until soft and remove the skin. Squeeze with the hand and discard the seed. Put the pulp through a sieve, pressing down with the back of a spoon. Add the sugar to the liquid. Taste and add more sugar if required. Put through a liquidizer if the texture is too thick. Leave to cool for 30 minutes. Add the milk and mix well. Leave to cool for a further 30 minutes. Stir and mix well before serving.

Lime sherbert

This drink is marvellous for hot summer days.

SERVES 2–4
juice of 3 limes
90–120 ml (6–8 tablespoons) sugar
900 ml (1½ pints) water

Mix the lime juice with the sugar, making sure the sugar is dissolved. Add the water and stir for 3–5 minutes. Chill. Serve with ice if desired.

Spicy tea

This delicately spiced tea is very warming (my mother always gave me this when I had a cold) and is a fragrant alternative to coffee for after the meal. It is best made with half milk and half water boiled together. Serve with or without sugar.

SERVES 2–4
300 ml (½ pint) milk
300 ml (½ pint) water
2 teabags
2 sticks cinnamon
3 whole cardamoms

Bring the milk and the water to the boil and add the teabags. Lower the heat, add the cinnamon sticks and whole cardamoms and bring back to the boil slowly. Allow to boil for 3–5 minutes. Strain into a tea-pot and discard the cinnamon sticks and cardamoms. Serve hot.

CHAPTER 16
Desserts

Indian meals usually end with something sweet, just as they do in the West. If you are serving an Indian dessert, which will probably be quite rich and very sweet, it is a good idea to offer a choice of fresh fruit – mangoes, guavas or melon, for example – as well. These are best served chilled, especially in the summer months.

Among Indian people desserts such as bread pudding (*shahi tukray*), carrot halva (*gagar ka halva*) and Indian vermicelli dessert (*sheer khorma*) are served only for special occasions, such as a religious festival, and some can be decorated with *varq*, the edible silver leaf which always signifies that there is something to celebrate.

In this section I have included some simple desserts such as Indian rice pudding (*chawal ki kheer*) as well as the more elaborate ones.

Do try some of these dishes. I find that because few restaurants offer much in the way of special Indian desserts they are usually a complete revelation to my Western guests – and always a pleasant one.

Chawal ki kheer
RICE PUDDING

We cook our rice pudding in a saucepan over a low heat rather than in the oven like the British version – which is also far less sweet. Rice pudding is one of the most popular of all desserts in Indian households.

SERVES 8–10
75 g (3 oz) basmati rice
1200 ml (2 pints) milk
120 ml (8 tablespoons) sugar
DECORATION
  varq *(silver leaf)*

Wash the rice. Bring to the boil in 1 pint (600 ml) milk over a very low heat. Cook until the milk has been absorbed by the rice. Remove from the heat. Mash the rice, preferably with a wooden masher, making swift, round movements in the pan, for at least 5 minutes. Return to the heat, gradually add the other pint (600 ml) milk and bring to the boil over a low heat, stirring occasionally. Add the sugar and continue stirring for about 7–10 minutes or until the *kheer* is quite thick in consistency. Transfer into a heatproof bowl. Decorate with *varq*. Serve on its own or with the *pooris* on page 141.

Shahi tukray
INDIAN BREAD PUDDING

This, the Indian equivalent of the English bread and butter pudding, is rather a special dessert, usually cooked for weddings or other special occasions.

SERVES 4–6
6 medium slices bread
75 ml (5 tablespoons) ghee (preferably pure)
150 ml (10 tablespoons) sugar
300 ml ($\frac{1}{2}$ pint) water
3 green cardamoms, without husks
600 ml (1 pint) milk
170 ml (6 fl oz) evaporated milk or khoya *(see below)*
2.5 ml ($\frac{1}{2}$ teaspoon) saffron strands
8 pistachio nuts, soaked, peeled and chopped
8–10 flaked almonds
2 leaves varq *(silver leaf)*

Cut the bread slices into quarters. Heat the ghee in a frying-pan and fry the bread slices until a crisp golden brown. Place in a heatproof dish and set aside. Make a thick syrup with the sugar, water and cardamom seeds. Boil until the syrup thickens and pour over the fried bread. In a separate saucepan bring to the boil the milk, evaporated milk or *khoya* and the saffron over a low heat until the milk has halved in volume. Pour over the bread. Decorate with the pistachios, flaked almonds and *varq*. Serve with or without cream.

Khoya
THICKENED MILK

900 ml (1$\frac{1}{2}$ pints) milk

In a large, heavy saucepan bring the milk to boil, watching carefully. Lower the heat and boil for 35–40 minutes, stirring occasionally. The milk should reduce to a quarter of its volume, and when completely cooked should resemble a sticky dough.

Use for making Indian desserts such as Indian bread pudding (*shahi tukray*).

Shakar kand ki kheer
SWEET POTATO DESSERT

This milky dessert can be eaten hot or cold.

SERVES 8–10
1 kg (2 lb) sweet potato
900 ml (1½ pints) milk
175 g (7 oz) sugar
a few flaked almonds to decorate

Peel the sweet potatoes. Wash and slice using a sharp knife. Place in a large saucepan, cover with 600 ml (1 pint) milk and cook slowly until the sweet potato is soft enough to be mashed (preferably a wooden masher). Remove from the heat and mash to remove all lumps, add the sugar and the remaining 300 ml (½ pint) milk, return to the heat and simmer until the mixture thickens. It should reach the consistency of a cream of chicken soup.

Decorate with flaked almonds.

Badaam ka halva
ALMOND DESSERT

Rich and mouth-watering, this dessert can be prepared in advance of the meal. It is served cold.

SERVES 4–6
75 g (3 oz) unsalted butter
200 g (8 oz) ground almonds
200 g (8 oz) sugar
150 ml (5 fl oz) single cream
8 almonds, soaked, peeled and chopped
10 pistachio nuts, soaked, peeled and chopped

In a medium-sized saucepan, preferably non-stick, melt the butter. Add the ground almonds, sugar and cream. Lower the heat and stir continuously for 10–12 minutes, scraping the bottom of the pan.

Increase the heat to turn the mixture a little darker in colour. Transfer the mixture to a shallow dish and smooth the top with the back of a spoon. Decorate the top with the almonds and pistachios, leave to set for about 1 hour, cut into diamond shapes and serve cold.

Gulab jamun
DEEP-FRIED SWEETMEAT IN SYRUP

This is one of the most popular Indian sweetmeats. 'Gulab' means rose and the flavour and beautiful aroma of this sweetmeat come from rose water. The finished dish can be served hot or cold and makes a delicious dinner-party dessert served with cream.

SERVES 6–8
75 ml (5 tablespoons) dried full-cream milk powder
22 ml (1½ tablespoons) plain flour
5 ml (1 teaspoon) baking powder
22 ml (1½ tablespoons) unsalted butter
1 medium egg
5 ml (1 teaspoon) milk to mix (if required)
150 ml (10 tablespoons) pure or vegetable ghee
SYRUP
  750 ml (1¼ pints) water
  120 ml (8 tablespoons) sugar
  2 green cardamoms, peeled, with seeds crushed
  1 large pinch saffron strands
  30 ml (2 tablespoons) rose water

Place all the dry ingredients in a bowl. Melt the butter. Whisk the egg. Add the butter and egg to the dry ingredients. Blend with a fork (and add the milk at this stage if necessary) to form a soft dough. Break the dough into about 12 small pieces and shape, in the palms of your hands, into small, smooth balls.

Heat the ghee in a deep-frying pan or *karahi*, lower the heat and start frying the balls about 3–4 at a time, tossing and turning gently with a slotted spoon until a dark golden brown. Remove from the pan and set aside in a deep bowl.

For the syrup, boil the water and sugar for 7–10 minutes. Add the crushed cardamom seeds and saffron, and pour over the *gulab jamuns*.

Pour the rose water sparingly on top. Allow about 10 minutes for the *gulab jamuns* to soak up some of the syrup.

Gajar ka halva
CARROT DESSERT

I remember the time, before food processors were invented, when my mother, who always believed in making such dishes as *gajar ka halva* in large quantities, made us children sit with about a pound of carrots each and a stainless steel hand grater to grate all the carrots. It was rather a boring task and my sister and I used to get told off for chatting rather than grating.

I like to use pure ghee for this halva as it is rather special and tastes better made with pure ghee. However, if you are trying to limit your fat intake, use vegetable ghee instead. Decorated with *varq* (silver leaf) and nuts, it makes a very impressive dinner-party dessert. It is best served warm, with fresh cream if desired, and can be made well in advance because it freezes very well.

SERVES 4–6
1.5 kg (3 lb) carrots
150 ml (10 tablespoons) ghee
600 ml (1 pint) milk
170 ml (6 fl oz) evaporated milk or khoya *(page 134)*
10 whole cardamoms, peeled and crushed
120–150 ml (8–10 tablespoons) sugar
25 g (1 oz) pistachio nuts, chopped
25 g (1 oz) flaked almonds
2 leaves varq *(silver leaf) (optional)*

Wash, peel and grate the carrots. Heat the ghee in a large, heavy saucepan. Add the grated carrots and stir-fry for 15–20 minutes or until the moisture from the carrots has evaporated and the carrots have darkened in colour. Add the milk, evaporated milk or *khoya*, cardamom and sugar to the carrots. Continue to stir-fry for a further 30–35 minutes, using the *bhoono*-ing method, until it is a rich brownish-red colour.

Transfer to a large shallow dish and decorate with the pistachio nuts, flaked almonds and *varq*.

Sooji ka halva
SEMOLINA DESSERT

This halva is eaten with *pooris* and potato curry (*aloo bhujia*) for breakfast in northern India. It makes a delicious and a filling brunch dish. If you like you can just have the halva with some fresh cream.

SERVES 4
90 ml (6 tablespoons) pure ghee
3 whole cloves
3 whole cardamoms
120 ml (8 tablespoons) coarse semolina
2.5 ml ($\frac{1}{2}$ teaspoon) saffron
50 g (2 oz) sultanas
150 ml (10 tablespoons) sugar
300 ml ($\frac{1}{2}$ pint) water
300 ml ($\frac{1}{2}$ pint) milk
DECORATION
   25 g (1 oz) desiccated coconut, roasted
   25 g (1 oz) flaked almonds
   25 g (1 oz) pistachio nuts, soaked and chopped

Melt the ghee in a medium saucepan. Add the cloves and cardamoms. Lower the heat. Add the semolina and stir-fry until it turns a little darker. Add the saffron, sultanas and the sugar. Mix in the water and milk and stir-fry continuously until the semolina is soft. Add more water if required. Remove from the heat, serve decorated with desiccated coconut, flaked almonds and pistachios.

Sheer khorma
INDIAN VERMICELLI PUDDING

Indian vermicelli (*seviyan*), which is very fine, is delicious cooked in milk and ghee. Muslims make this for one of their religious festivals called Eid, which is celebrated at the end of Ramadan, the month of fasting. *Sheer khorma* can be eaten hot or cold. My mother always makes it in a large quantity and leaves it in the centre of the table in a large punch bowl on Eid, and we – and our guests – help ourselves to it all day long.

SERVES 4–6
25g (1oz) pistachio nuts, finely chopped
25g (1oz) flaked almonds, finely chopped
45ml (3 tablespoons) ghee
100g (4oz) seviyan *(Indian vermicelli)*
900ml (1½ pints) milk
170ml (6fl oz) evaporated milk
120ml (8 tablespoons) sugar
6 dates, stoned and dried

Soak the pistachio nuts for at least 3 hours, peel and dice thinly and leave aside with the flaked almonds. Melt the ghee in a large saucepan and lightly fry the *seviyan*. Immediately turn the heat lower (the *seviyan* will turn golden brown very quickly so be careful not to burn them), and if necessary remove from the heat (do not worry if some bits are a little darker than others). Add the milk and bring to the boil slowly, taking care that it does not boil over. Add the evaporated milk, sugar and the stoned dates. Allow to simmer for about 10 minutes, without a lid, stirring occasionally. When the consistency starts to thicken, pour it in a serving bowl and decorate with the pistachio nuts and flaked almonds. Serve in bowls.

Badaam ka sherbert
ALMOND SHERBERT

I prefer to use whole almonds rather than already ground almonds for this dish as I find they give it a better texture.

SERVES 2
225g (8oz) whole almonds
30ml (2 tablespoons) sugar
300ml (½ pint) milk
300ml (½ pint) water

Soak the almonds overnight or for a minimum of 3 hours. Peel the almonds and grind to a fine paste in a food processor. Add the sugar and grind once again to blend the sugar and almonds to a fine paste. Add the milk and water. Mix well, in a liquidizer if you have one. Leave to chill for 30 minutes in a refrigerator. Stir and serve.

Badaam ke lauze
ALMOND SLICES

A mouthwatering dessert that is sure to impress your guests, especially if served with whipped cream, this can be made a day or even a week in advance and re-heated. It freezes beautifully.

SERVES 6–8
3 medium eggs
75g (3oz) ground almonds
200g (8oz) milk powder
200g (8oz) sugar
2.5ml (½ teaspoon) saffron strands
100g (4oz) unsalted butter
25g (1oz) flaked almonds

Beat the eggs in a bowl and leave aside. Place the ground almonds, milk powder, sugar and saffron in a large mixing bowl and mix well. Melt the butter in a small saucepan, pour over the dry ingredients and mix well with a fork. Add the beaten eggs and blend. Spread the mixture in a shallow 15–20-cm (7–9-inch) dish and bake in a pre-heated oven at 160°C, 325°F, Gas 3 for 45 minutes. Check whether cooked by piercing with a knife or a skewer, which will emerge clean if it is done. Cut into diamond shapes and decorate with flaked almonds.

This dish is best eaten hot but may also be served cold.

Badaam ka hareera
GROUND ALMONDS COOKED IN GHEE & MILK

Traditionally served at breakfast, this almond-based dish is said to sharpen the mind. It can be served on its own, with *paratas* or with toast and would make a good addition to any brunch menu. It is very quick to make.

SERVES 2–4
30ml (2 tablespoons) vegetable or pure ghee
25g (1oz) plain flour
100g (4oz) ground almonds
300ml (½ pint) milk
50g (2oz) sugar

Melt the ghee in a small saucepan. Lower the heat. Add the plain flour and stir vigorously to remove lumps. Add the almonds and keep stirring. Gradually add the milk and sugar and bring to the boil. Continue cooking for 3–5 minutes or until the liquid reaches the consistency of cream of chicken soup. Serve hot.

Pistay ka halva
PISTACHIO DESSERT

Rather an attractive-looking dessert, especially when decorated with *varq*, this is another dish that can be prepared in advance. It is delicious served with cream.

SERVES 4–6
900 ml (1½ pints) water
250 g (10 oz) pistachio nuts
250 g (10 oz) full-cream dried milk
450 g (1 lb) sugar
2 cardamoms, with seeds crushed
30 ml (2 tablespoons) rose water
250 g (1 oz) flaked almonds
a few strands saffron
600 ml (1 leaf) varq *(silver leaf) (optional)*

Boil about 1 pint (600 ml) water in a saucepan. Turn off the heat and soak the pistachios in this water for about 5 minutes. Drain and remove the skins. Grind the pistachios in a food processor, add the dried milk powder and mix well.

In a non-stick saucepan make the syrup by using 300 ml (½ pint) water and sugar; when the liquid begins to thicken add the crushed cardamom seeds, rose water and saffron. Add to the pistachio mixture and stir until the mixture thickens (about 5 minutes). Spread in a shallow dish and cut into diamond shapes. Decorate with flaked almonds and *varq* and leave to set.

Firni

GROUND RICE PUDDING

The rice is coarsely ground for this pudding and, like most Indian food, is cooked on top of the cooker. It makes a delicious dinner-party dessert, served cold.

SERVES 4–6
75 g (3 oz) coarsely ground rice
900 ml (1½ pints) milk
2 cardamom seeds, crushed
105 ml (7 tablespoons) sugar
5 ml (1 teaspoon) kevra *water*
DECORATION
   6–8 pistachio nuts, coarsely ground
   varq *(silver leaf) (optional)*

If the rice is not already coarsely ground, grind it in a food processor. Wash the rice at least twice, and place in a medium-sized saucepan with 600 ml (1 pint) milk and the crushed cardamom seeds. Cook over a very low heat for about 35–40 minutes, stirring occasionally.

Add the sugar and the other 300 ml (½ pint) milk and cook for a further 10 minutes, stirring occasionally. Sprinkle over the *kevra* water and pour into a serving dish.

Sprinkle the pistachio nuts thinly on top of the *firni*, either in a criss-cross pattern or just in the centre. Decorate with the *varq*.

Pooris stuffed with chana dhaal halva

In India this elaborate dish is made only once a year, for a religious festival which takes place during the lunar month of Rajab. We used to make it during the night with a group of relatives to eat the next morning. Some of us would make the pastry, others would roll it out and someone else would be busy frying in a large *karahi*. Before sunrise we would clear up and set out two large earthenware bowls containing the *pooris* and two others containing the rice pudding (*chawal ki kheer*) that always accompanied it. From about 9 o'clock guests would start arriving to sample what we had been making all night. It may sound like a lot of work, but for us children, in particular, it was great fun to be up all night with our cousins and friends — and, after all, it was only once a year.

For the *pooris* I use a combination of plain flour and semolina, which is very unusual but produces a delicious pastry. This is filled with chana dhaal halva (see below), deep-fried and served with the rice pudding. The *pooris* freeze well so it pays to make a large quantity and re-heat them in the oven. They can also be eaten cold, on their own. Allow two per person.

MAKES 10–12
200 g (8 oz) coarse semolina
100 g (4 oz) plain flour
2.5 ml (½ teaspoon) salt
22 ml (1½ tablespoons) ghee
150 ml (¼ pint) milk

Place the coarse semolina, plain flour and salt in a large mixing bowl and mix together. Add the ghee and rub in with your fingers. Gradually add the milk to form a soft dough. Knead for about 5 minutes with the back of your hand, cover and leave aside for about 3 hours. Take the dough out of the bowl, place on a lightly floured surface and knead for a further 15 minutes. Roll out into a 25-cm (10-inch) piece of dough and divide into ten equal portions. Roll out each of these into 12.5-cm (5-inch) circles and place the chana dhaal halva on one half of the rolled-out pastry. Dampen the edges with water and fold the other half over to seal the edges. Either make a pattern on the edges or simply pinch the pastry lightly.

When all the *pooris* are made, heat the ghee in a *karahi* or heavy frying-pan and fry the *pooris* on a low heat until golden brown. Place the *pooris* on a tray with some kitchen paper to drain. Serve with rice pudding (*chawal ki kheer*) or on their own.

Zarda
SWEET SAFFRON RICE

Zarda is a traditional dessert which is quick and easy to make and looks very impressive, especially decorated with pistachio nuts and *varq*.

SERVES 4
200 g (8 oz) basmati rice
200 g (8 oz) sugar
1 pinch saffron
300 ml ($\frac{1}{2}$ pint) water
30 ml (2 tablespoons) ghee
3 cloves
3 cardamoms
25 g (1 oz) sultanas
DECORATION
   a few pistachio nuts
   varq *(silver leaf)*

Wash the rice twice and bring to the boil. Remove from the heat when half-cooked, drain and leave aside. In a separate saucepan boil the sugar and saffron in 300 ml ($\frac{1}{2}$ pint) water and boil until the syrup thickens. Leave aside. In another saucepan heat the ghee, cloves and cardamoms. Remove from the heat. Return the rice to a low heat, add the sultanas and pour the syrup over the rice. Stir and mix. Pour the ghee over the rice and simmer over a low heat for 10–15 minutes. Check to see whether the rice is cooked; if not, add a little water, cover and simmer.

Serve warm decorated with pistachio nuts and *varq*, with cream if desired.

Kopray ki mithai
COCONUT SWEET

Quick and easy to make, this sweet is very similar to coconut ice. Pink colouring may be added towards the end if desired.

SERVES 4–6
75 g (3 oz) butter
200 g (8 oz) desiccated coconut
170 ml (6 fl oz) condensed milk
a few drops colouring (optional)

Melt the butter in a saucepan. Add the desiccated coconut, stir in the condensed milk and colouring and mix continuously for 7–10 minutes. Remove from the heat, spread in a shallow dish and leave to set for about 1 hour. Cut into diamond shapes and serve.

Chanay ki dhaal ka halva
CHANA DHAAL DESSERT

This is a very old recipe handed down to me by my mother. As described above, we used to make a special type of *poori* to stuff with this halva; accompanied by rice pudding (*chawal ki kheer*), these made a delectable snack. However, served on its own decorated with a few almond flakes, the halva makes a tasty dessert and will freeze well in or out of the *pooris*.

SERVES 4–6
120 ml (8 tablespoons) chana dhaal
900 ml (1½ pints) water
75 ml (5 tablespoons) ghee
2 green cardamoms, peeled
4 cloves
120 ml (8 tablespoons) sugar
30 ml (2 tablespoons) ground almonds
2.5 ml (½ teaspoon) saffron strands
50 g (2 oz) sultanas

If time allows, soak the chana dhaal for at least 3 hours. Wash twice. Place in a medium-sized saucepan and boil in 750 ml (1½ pints) water over a medium heat until all the water has evaporated and the *dhaal* is soft enough to be mashed into a paste.

In a separate large saucepan heat up the ghee and add the cardamom seeds and cloves. Lower the heat and add the chana dhaal paste and start stirring and mixing, using the *bhoono*-ing method. Stir, scraping the bottom of the pan, for about 5–7 minutes. Gradually fold in the sugar and ground almonds and continue *bhoono*-ing for 10 minutes. Add the saffron and sultanas and blend together. By now the halva should have thickened. Continue stirring for a further 5 minutes. Remove from the heat and transfer to a serving dish. Decorate with the flaked almonds.

Serve hot or cold with cream or stuffed in *pooris*.

Index